best | designed

Martin Nicholas Kunz . Michelle Galindo

modular houses

avedition

contents

introduction | design meets pre-fabricated houses

best designed modular houses is engaged in the growing popularity of architectural examination of all the aspects concerning modular construction. A topic which most people associate with boring or even bourgeois pre-fabricated houses. However, this collection shows approximately 40 current projects and sketches of ideas which demonstrate how good design can take form in only a few days. It demonstrates how it is possible to adapt construction to an individual lifestyle using industrially pre-fabricated elements and light materials.

There is a long history of pre-fabricated construction systems. They catered primarily to time-effective, cost-effective construction of houses. In 1624 panelized wood houses were shipped from England to Cape Ann, Massachusetts to provide housing for a fishing fleet. There was a great demand for houses which were able to be constructed quickly during the California gold rush when modular houses were shipped by railway freight cars. The breakthrough for industrially pre-fabricated houses came with industrialization and, of

course, Henry Ford's T-Model as a symbol for a high quality mass-produced item. In the late 30s and again in the late 60s famous designers developed an interest in this topic. Among these were: Le Corbusier, Walter Gropius, Jean Prouvé, Abert Frey, Buckminster Fuller, Charles and Ray Eames were concerned with developing mass-produced and affordable homes for everyone and designed construction segments under the consideration of industrial aesthetics. Walter Gropius founded his own pre-fabricated home company in the USA with his partners.

After years of creative wasteland, function and design are reunited again today. This union meets the concerns of the growing global need for flexibility and availability. For some years, architects and designers have increasingly concentrated on experimental freedom, which this genre offers and also permits. In the meanwhile, it is almost part of the standard architectural repertoire to present such examples that define homes of the future.

Projects can be discovered in this book in which one would like to move in right away. And that with a good conscience too, they use almost entirely environmentally-friendly materials. And they work in their construction of intelligent systems which, given a few exceptions, are truly affordable, in many cases can also be rebuilt on other locations. Projects such as the Loftcube—a transparent living cube—lend themselves as a site for modern nomads on the rooftops of metropolises. Whereas other models offer living close to nature, be it in the desert, forests or in the mountains. Man's necessities for living have been adapted to a new world and architecture is adapting to new ideas for building living spaces. Walter Gropius once spoke of "a new architecture for a new age."

Michelle Galindo

introduction | design trifft auf fertighaus

best designed modular houses befasst sich mit der immer populärer werdenden Architektur-Auseinandersetzung rund um modulares Bauen. Ein Thema, das die meisten mit langweiligen oder gar spießigen Fertighäusern verbinden. Diese Sammlung zeigt hingegen rund 40 aktuelle Projekte und Ideenskizzen, die demonstrieren wie auch gutes Design in wenigen Tagen Gestalt annehmen kann. Es legt dar, wie mit dem Einsatz von industriell vorgefertigten Elementen und leichten Materialien ein an individuelle Lebensbedürfnisse angepasstes Bauen möglich ist.

Es gibt eine lange Geschichte von Fertighaussystemen. Überwiegend waren sie darauf ausgerichtet einen zeit- und kosteneffizienten Hausbau zu ermöglichen. 1624 wurden bereits Häuser aus Holzbauteilen von England nach Cape Ann in Massachusetts verschifft um dort eine Fischereisiedlung aufzubauen. Einen großen Bedarf an schnell zu errichtendem Wohnraum gab es mit dem Goldrausch in Kalifornien. Auf Güterzügen wurden Baukastenhäuser an die Westküste transportiert. Mit der Industrialisierung und nicht zuletzt Henry Fords T-Modell als Symbol für eine

hochwertige Massenproduktion kam schließlich der Durchbruch für industriell vorgefertigte Wohngebäude. In den 30er und in den 60er Jahren haben schließlich auch bekannte Entwerfer das Thema für sich entdeckt: u.a. Le Corbusier, Walter Gropius, Albert Frey, Buckminster Fuller, Charles und Ray Eames beschäftigten sich mit serienfähigen und kostengünstigen Heimen für jedermann und entwarfen Hausbauelemente unter Berücksichtigung einer industriellen Ästhetik. Walter Gropius gründete in den USA mit Partnern sogar eine eigene Fertighausfirma.

Nach Jahren der gestalterischen Ödnis bilden Funktion und Design heute wieder eine Einheit, die dem wachsenden globalen Bedürfnis nach Flexibilität und Verfügbarkeit Rechnung trägt. Seit einigen Jahren konzentrieren sich Architekten und Designer vermehrt auf die experimentellen Freiheiten, die dieses Genre bietet und auch zulässt. Inzwischen gehört es sogar fast zum Bestandteil eines architektonischen Werkberichts, solche Beispiele zu präsentieren, die zukünftige Wohnräume bestimmen.

In dem Buch sind Projekte zu entdecken, in die man am liebsten sofort einziehen würde. Und das auch noch mit gutem Gewissen, nutzen sie doch fast durchweg umweltverträgliche Materialien. Und sie bedienen sich in ihrer Konstruktion intelligenter Systeme, die bis auf wenige Ausnahmen wirklich kostengünstig sind, in vielen Fällen können sie auch an anderer Stelle wiederaufgebaut werden. Projekte wie der Loftcube – eine transparente Wohnschachtel – empfehlen sich als Stätte für das Nomadendasein auf den Dächern der Metropolen. Während andere

Modelle das Leben in der Natur anbieten, sei dies in Wüsten, Wäldern oder auf Bergen. Die Lebens- und Wohnbedürfnisse der Menschen haben sich bereits einer neuen Welt angepasst und die Architektur zieht mit neuen Wohnbauideen nach. Walter Gropius sprach einmal von „einer neuen Architektur für ein neues Zeitalter".

Michelle Galindo

haus trüb | horgen . switzerland

DESIGN: agps architecture (Marc Angélil, Sarah Graham, Manuel Scholl, Reto Pfenninger, Hanspeter Oester)

The design of Haus Trüb took inspiration from conceptual artist Gordon Matta-Clark who enlisted remnants from abandoned buildings. In his method of art making, Matta-Clark sought out a culinary analogy. He experimented with the application of three culinary operations including "Selection" whereby ingredients are separated from their settings; "Preparation" in which each substance undergoes a variety of transformations; and "Cooking" which includes the elements of flame and time utilized in such techniques as charring or sautéing. From these methods, agps Architecture defined the rudiments of space, volume, site, organization, and construction for Haus Trüb. The method culminates in a unique design marked by a horizontal exterior volume which, by and large, relies on a modernist language.

Extensive glazed areas on the home's exterior unveil a space which has been sliced up inside, thereby revealing the application of Matta-Clark's train of thought.

Das Design von Haus Trüb wurde durch den Konzeptionskünstler Gordon Matta-Clark inspiriert, der Überreste herrenloser Gebäude wiederverwendete. Für seine Methode, Kunst zu machen, suchte Matta-Clark eine kulinarische Parallele. Er experimentierte mit der Anwendung dreier Arbeitsvorgänge beim Kochen, der „Auswahl", bei der die Zutaten aus ihrer Verpackung genommen werden, der „Vorbereitung", bei der jede Zutat eine Reihe von Veränderungen durchläuft, und dem „Kochen", bei dem Elemente wie Feuer und Zeit für Techniken wie das Anbraten und das Sautieren genutzt werden. Basierend auf diesen Methoden definierten die Architekten von agps architecture ihre Ansätze für Raum, Umfang, Aufstellungsort, Organisation und Konstruktion von Haus Trüb. Diese Vorgehensweise führte zu einem einzigartigen Design, das sich durch ein horizontales äußeres Bauvolumen auszeichnet, das, im Großen und Ganzen, auf einer modernistischen Formensprache beruht. Ausgedehnte verglaste Flächen an der Fassade des Hauses machen einen unterteilten Innenraum sichtbar, der die Umsetzung von Matta-Clarks Gedankengang zeigt.

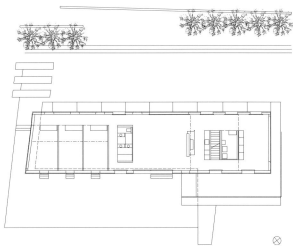

loftcube | berlin . germany

DESIGN: Studio Aisslinger, Werner Aisslinger

With the loftcube, the architect and designer, Werner Aisslinger, from Berlin has created an ideal concept for big city nomads. This modern, transparent cube suggests a nomadic life on the roofs of the big cities of the world. Berlin is exemplary for this new model with its numerous buildings made of prefabricated concrete slabs, whose flat roofs are the ideal foundation for this modern architecture. The relatively light weight of the "flying" cube enable problem-free transportation to and from by crane or helicopter. The loftcube allows two different accommodation concepts: use as a tenant or as an owner. Tenants can reserve the fixed "rooftop apartment" with an unobstructed view of the city for a temporary stay. The owner on the other hand can dock his/her loftcube on stations designed especially for this purpose. The basics of the minimalist design are a steel frame construction and large windows. Materials and colors of the organic modules are variable and the area of 11.6 x 11.6 inch can be subdivided as desired using wall panels. The loftcube could keep changing the skyline of a city through this new form of "mobile" settlement.

Ein ideales Konzept für Großstadtnomaden hat der Berliner Architekt und Designer Werner Aisslinger mit seinem Loftcube kreiert. Dieser moderne, transparente Kubus suggeriert ein Nomadenleben auf den Dächern der Großstädte dieser Welt. Beispielhaft für das neue Modell steht Berlin mit seinen unzähligen Plattenbauten, deren Flachdächer das ideale Fundament für diese neuzeitliche Architektur sind. Das verhältnismäßig leichte Gewicht des „fliegenden" Kubus macht den problemlosen An- und Abtransport durch Hochbaukran oder Hubschrauber möglich. Der Loftcube erlaubt zwei unterschiedliche Unterbringungskonzepte: die Nutzung als Mieter oder als Eigentümer. Mieter können die fest installierte „Dachwohnung" mit unverbautem Blick über die Stadt für einen vorübergehenden Aufenthalt buchen. Der Eigentümer hingegen dockt seinen Loftcube an eigens dafür vorgesehene Stationen an. Das Grundgerüst des minimalistischen Designs sind eine Stahlrahmenkonstruktion und große Glasfenster. Materialien und Farben des organisch geschwungenen Moduls sind variabel und die Fläche von gut 7 auf 7 Meter ist durch Wandpaneele nach Wunsch unterteilbar. Durch diese neue Form der „losen" Besiedelung könnte der Loftcube die Skyline einer Stadt immer wieder verändern.

weehouse | st. paul, mn . usa

DESIGN: Alchemy Architects

Exceptionally versatile, weehouses offer an efficient and low cost alternative to traditional prefabricated homes. Factory assembled, their short fabrication time eliminated high construction costs associated with custom building. Because they are intended for any climate, they are not only built from durable materials, but sustainable ones as well. Clients can modify a basic modular system to change or integrate variable aspects of the house from windows and stairs to finishes and details. Such flexibility means that weehouses can be used for a variety of purposes, whether as a home or office. The only prerequisite is that the intended site be accessible by the truck delivering the house. Once there, client and contractor are responsible for providing the foundation, utility connections, and final preparations to the modules. Not only can these homes be reassembled on other sites, but the modular system also allows the clients to enlarge the house to accommodate unforeseeable needs in the future.

Das weehouse ist außergewöhnlich vielseitig und bietet eine gut durchdachte und preisgünstige Alternative zu den traditionellen Fertigteilhäusern. Durch die industrielle Vorfertigung ist nur eine kurze Bauzeit notwendig, was die hohen Kosten, die normalerweise bei einem speziell angefertigten Gebäude anfallen, drastisch reduziert. Da sie für jedes Klima geeignet sein sollen, werden die weehouses nicht nur aus haltbaren, sondern auch aus umweltverträglichen Materialien errichtet. Der Kunde kann je nach Wunsch ein Basissystem von Modulen variieren, indem er verschiedene Teile des Hauses austauscht oder integriert, von Fenstern und Treppen über den Innenausbau bis zu einzelnen Details. Diese Flexibilität macht es möglich, das weehouse zu verschiedensten Zwecken zu nutzen, ob nun als Wohnraum oder Büro. Einzige Voraussetzung ist, dass das vorgesehene Baugelände für den Lieferwagen, der das Haus transportiert, erreichbar ist. Nach Lieferung ist der Kunde und Auftraggeber für das Fundament, alle Versorgungsanschlüsse und die letzten Vorbereitungen der Module verantwortlich. Diese Häuser können nicht nur an anderen Standorten wieder aufgebaut werden, das modulare System erlaubt es dem Bauherren, das Haus jederzeit zu vergrößern, um nicht vorhersehbaren Raumbedarf jederzeit zu decken.

haus der gegenwart | münchen . germany
DESIGN: Allmann Sattler Wappner . Architekten

Giving simple answers to difficult questions was the goal of the archi-tects, Allmann Sattler Wappner, from Munich, Germany when designing a flexible house for a family of four. The design was supposed to fulfill two apparently conflictive requirements of our time: the desire for pri-vate space as well as the need for openness and greater flexibility. The interplay and symbiosis between nature and architecture was also the subject on the premises neighboring the Riemer Park in Munich. On the exterior of the building, a continuous hedge was used as a formulating element. It defines and separates entrances and paths along the square property and allocates each of the three rooms on the ground floor a small private area. Furthermore, every room has its own private entrance. The ceilings are made of wooden terraces on the upper floor. The com-mon room is located optically floating above the landscape: the spatial center of the building with areas for cooking, living and media are defined by staircases. There is an open room located beneath the common room which can be used as a garage, forecourt, and outdoor hobby room. Contemporary materials such as wood, glass, cement, and the constant intervening of the "front lawn hedge" characterize the unusual of form this flexible house.

Einfache Antworten auf schwierige Fragen zu geben, das war das Anliegen der Architekten Allmann Sattler Wappner aus München bei ihrem Entwurf eines flexiblen Wohnhauses für einen 4-Personen-Haushalt. Der Entwurf sollte zwei scheinbar gegensätzliche Anforderungen unserer Zeit erfüllen: den Wunsch nach Privatsphäre und Rückzugsmöglichkeit sowie den Drang nach Offenheit und großer Flexibilität. Auch das Wechselspiel und die Symbiose zwischen Natur und Architektur werden auf einem Grundstück am Rande des Riemer Parks in München thematisiert. Im Außenraum des Gebäudes dient eine fortlaufende Hecke als formulierendes Element. Sie definiert und gliedert Zugänge und Wege auf dem quadratischen Grundstück und weist den 3 Wohnräumen im Erdgeschoss jeweils kleine private Bereiche zu. Jeder Wohnraum hat außerdem einen eigenen Eingang. Die Decken bilden hölzerne Terrassen im Obergeschoss, wo sich, über dem Landschaftshorizont optisch schwebend, die Kollektivbox befindet: das räumliche Zentrum des Gebäudes, dessen Bereiche für Kochen, Wohnen und Medien durch die Treppenauf-gänge definiert werden. Unter der Box befindet sich ein offener Raum, der als Garage, Vorplatz und Hobbyraum im Freien dient. Zeitgenössische Materialien wie Holz, Glas, Beton und die stetige Intervenierung der „Vorgartenhecke" prägen die ungewöhnliche Formensprache dieses flexiblen Wohnhauses.

living box | küblis . switzerland
DESIGN: ARCHITEAM 4 Basel

"The Living Box grows with your family—up to a maximum of 79 children." The architects advertise for their energy-saving houses and super energy-efficient houses with this slogan. Large window fronts to the south allow sufficient daylight into the house, on the north side of the house appears more enclosed and there is an intentional use of artificial light. A cleverly-designed system directs, accumulates, and uses the sun's energy in the house for optimal use. The basis of the pre-fabricated wooden module houses are wooden supports and ceiling elements. The wall and window modules can be built as desired on the supporting framework. The model for this style of construction was Le Corbusier's 5-point system. This permits the maximum freedom in the floor plan layout and construction can be expanded in all directions; according to the motto: where do you want to go today? There are practically no restrictions to the number of inhabitants and the form of living together. In addition to cement, glass, and chrome, wood dominates the structure not only on the façade but also in the interior. Houses have been built in this manner for almost 10 years, integrating the latest developments and understanding about the use of solar energy.

„Die Living Box wächst mit Ihrer Familie – bis zu maximal 79 Kindern." Mit diesem Slogan werben die Architekten für ihr Niedrigenergie- bzw. Minergiehaus. Große Fensterflächen nach Süden hin lassen ausreichend Tageslicht in das Gebäude, auf der Nordseite ist der Bau optisch eher geschlossen und es wird gezielt mit Kunstlicht gearbeitet. Eine ausgeklügelte Systematik leitet, speichert und verwertet die Sonnenenergie im Gebäude, sodass sie optimal genutzt wird. Basis des vorgefertigten Holzbaukastens sind Holzstützen und Deckenelemente. An dieses Trageskelett werden frei kombinierbare Wand- und Fenstermodule angebracht. Als Vorbild für diese Bauweise diente Le Corbusiers 5-Punkte-System. Dies erlaubt eine größtmögliche Freiheit in der Grundrissgestaltung und der Bau lässt sich in alle Richtungen ausweiten, frei nach dem Motto: Wohin geht's heute? Dadurch sind der Bewohneranzahl und der Form des Zusammenlebens fast keine Grenzen gesetzt. Neben Beton, Glas und Chromstahl dominiert in erster Linie Holz, sowohl an der Fassade wie auch im Innenraum. Seit fast 10 Jahren werden Häuser in dieser Weise gebaut, wobei immer die neuesten Entwicklungen und Erkenntnisse über die Nutzung von Sonnenenergie mit einfließen.

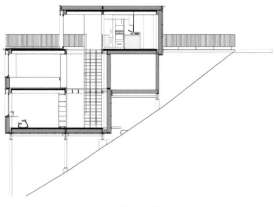

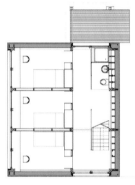

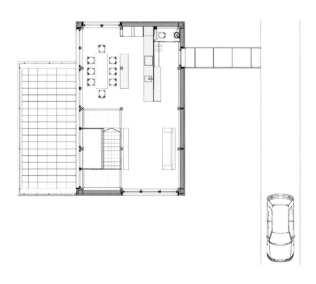

weberhaus option | rheinau-linx . germany
DESIGN: Bauart Architekten und Planer AG

"The house that I would like would consist of one large room in which one could talk with friends in one corner, eat in another, sleep in another and work in another" this quote by William Morris best explains the unusual concept of the WeberHaus Option. Originally constructed as an addition to an existing building, the house with its appealing construction style can also be used as an independent living cube. Based on the Modular-T system of the architects, Bauart, from Bern, Switzerland, a maximally-optimized living space is created here in minimum space. The stipulation for the development of the building elements was to bring together high standards, extraordinary design, low costs and optimum use of space. A centrally located supply grid and a straight set of stairs are surrounded by freely-definable living space. On the ground floor there are the offices; on the upper floor are the private living room and bedrooms. The façade has a large window opening in every direction and therefore has a sculptural character. The house is built completely of wood and generously insulated, which creates a comfortable room climate.

„Das Haus, das mir gefallen würde, bestünde aus einem großen Raum, in dem man in einer Ecke mit seinen Freunden redet, in einer anderen isst, in einer anderen schläft und einer anderen arbeitet" – dieses Zitat von William Morris erklärt das ungewöhnliche Konzept des WeberHauses Option am besten. Hauptsächlich als Ergänzungsbau für bestehende Gebäude und Anlagen konzipiert, kann das Haus mit seiner ansprechenden Bauweise auch als eigenständiger Wohnkubus genutzt werden. Basierend auf dem System Modular-T der Architekten Bauart aus Bern wird hier auf minimalem Raum ein maximal optimierter Wohnraum geschaffen. Maßgabe bei der Entwicklung der Bauelemente war der Anspruch, außergewöhnliches Design, geringe Kosten und optimale Raumnutzung unter einen Hut zu bekommen. Ein zentral gelegener Versorgungskern und eine einläufige Treppe werden von frei definierbaren Wohnflächen umgeben. Im Erdgeschoss befinden sich die Gemeinschaftsräume, im Obergeschoss private Wohn- und Schlafräume. Die Fassade weist in jeder Himmelsrichtung eine große Fensteröffnung auf und hat dadurch einen skulpturalen Charakter. Das Haus ist konsequent in Holz gebaut und großzügig gedämmt, was für ein angenehmes Raumklima sorgt.

the retreat | london . uk
DESIGN: Buckley Gray Yeoman

Retreat Homes Limited is a concept by the British architects, Buckley Gray Yeoman. They took the topic of living while on vacation, to be more specific, the camper-trailer, and developed such a highly-polished solution that one can speak of a second home or summer residence rather than the classic camper-trailer. The construction style is modular and therefore affordable. Retreat Homes is available in various sizes, can be transported, is flexible and entices with all its comforts that standard homes offer. Numerous varieties are offered with regard to the layout of the rooms, for example with built-in closets, additional bedroom or integrated bath. One possible variant separates the living room and bedrooms in order to avoid conflicting interests between rest and activity; this is emphasized by an outdoor terrace located between them. The trailer is made exclusively in high quality wood, for example oak for the floors, teak for the kitchen furnishings and hardwoods for the window frames. The glass windows reach all the way to the floor and ensure sufficient daylight even in the winter months. The architects avoided materials such as plastic or chemical surface treatment; instead they used materials which are as natural as possible, which are also 100 per cent recyclable.

Retreat Homes limited ist ein Konzept der britischen Architekten Buckley Gray Yeoman. Sie nahmen sich des Themas Wohnen im Urlaub an, genauer gesagt dem Wohnwagen, und haben eine Lösung entwickelt, die so ausgefeilt ist, dass man eher von einem Zweitwohnsitz, Sommerdomizil oder Gartenhäuschen sprechen kann als vom klassischen Wohnanhänger. Die Bauweise ist modular und daher erschwinglich. Retreat Homes ist in verschiedenen Größen erhältlich, transportabel, flexibel und lockt mit allen Annehmlichkeiten, die auch das eigene Heim bietet. Unzählige Spielarten werden hinsichtlich der Raumgliederung angeboten, etwa mit Einbauschrank, zusätzlichem Schlafraum oder integriertem Bad. Eine mögliche Variante trennt Wohn- und Schlafbereich, um den Interessenkonflikt zwischen Ruhe und Aktivität zu vermeiden; betont wird dies durch die dazwischen liegende Außenterrasse. Der Ferienwagen ist ausschließlich in qualitativ hochwertigem Holz gefertigt, beispielsweise wurde Eiche für den Boden, Teak für die Küchenmöbel und Hartholz bei den Fensterrahmen verwendet. Die Glasfenster reichen bis zum Boden und garantieren auch in den Wintermonaten eine ausreichende Versorgung mit Sonnenlicht. Materialien wie Plastik oder chemische Oberflächenbehandlung haben die Architekten vermieden, stattdessen werden möglichst naturbelassene Werkstoffe verwendet, die zu 100 Prozent recycelbar sind.

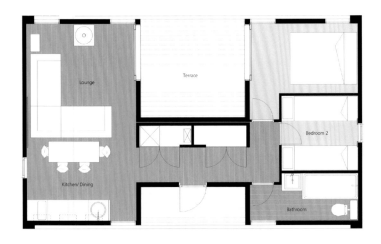

murray grove apartments | london . uk
DESIGN: Cartwright Pickard Architects

The Murray Grove Apartment Building on the southeastern edge of the city of London stands on a corner property in an exposed location. It is England's first multi-story affordable housing scheme to be built off-site. Made of steel-framed modules, it was assembled in only 6 months at its present location with help of a crane. The pre-fabrication of the building segments saves time, ensuring a fast occupation, which made it cost-effective, an absolute necessity considering the rising property costs, especially in the London area. Thus, it is not only possible in this manner to provide affordable housing space for singles, young couples, or communal residence, but also for families. The design by Cartwright Pickard Architects was also convincing because the 5-story apartment building did not necessarily look like a "socialized project". Each of the 30 units has a balcony, extensive windows, and glass doors on the courtyard side, which ensure sufficient daylight. Terracotta tiles were used on the street elevation for exterior decoration. The central tower, which reflects the contemporary, technically-innovative building, is used as a foyer with elevators and stairwell.

Das Murray-Grove-Apartmentgebäude am südöstlichen Stadtrand von London steht auf einem Eckgrundstück in exponierter Lage. Es ist Englands erstes Hochhaus mit diesem erschwinglichen Bebauungssystem, das außerhalb der Baustelle gefertigt wird. Es besteht aus Stahlträgermodulen, die in nur 6 Monaten an seinem heutigen Standort mithilfe eines Krans errichtet wurden. Die Vorfertigung der Bauteile in der Produktion spart Zeit, garantiert einen schnellen Bezug und macht es wiederum rentabel, was bei steigenden Grundstückspreisen vor allem im Londoner Stadtgebiet unbedingt notwendig ist. So ist es möglich, erschwinglichen Wohnraum nicht nur für Einzelpersonen, junge Paare oder Wohngemeinschaften bereitzustellen, sondern auch Familien. Der Entwurf des Architekturbüros Cartwright Pickard Architects überzeugt aber auch deshalb, weil dem 5-stöckigen Wohngebäude sein „sozialer Auftrag" nicht zwangsläufig anzusehen ist. Jede der 30 Wohneinheiten verfügt über einen Fertigteilbalkon, großflächige Fenster und verglaste Türen auf der Hofseite, die für ausreichend Tageslicht sorgen. Terrakottakacheln werden in Höhe des Erdgeschoßes zu Außenverkleidung genutzt. Der zentrale Turm, der die zeitgemäße, technisch innovative Gebäudestruktur reflektiert, dient als Eingangsbereich und Verteiler mit Aufzügen und Treppenhaus.

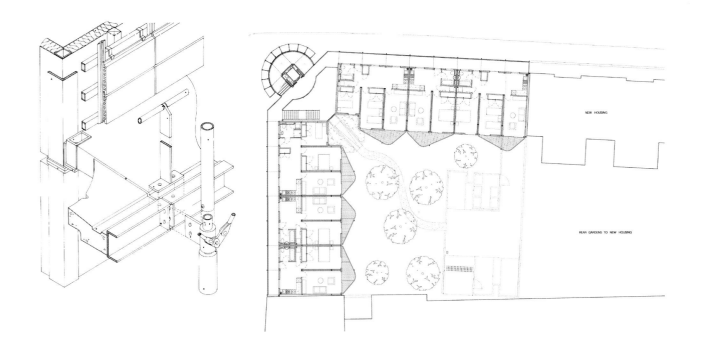

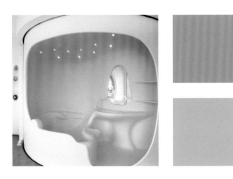

hanse-colani-rotorhaus | oberleichtersbach . germany
DESIGN: Luigi Colani

Here the name is the program. A rotating system constitutes the heart and center of this extraordinary design by Luigi Colani. The designer, whose calling card is the language of organic form and whose design intentionally distinguishes itself from today's straight-lined architecture, wanted to attain maximum living space for minimum outside dimension. With its floor space of 6 x 6 meters, the rotating house is appealing to both singles and small families. In the core of the Colani house are three function areas—bedrooms, kitchen and bath—united in a revolving system and, according to how it is used, can be entered merely by pressing a button. Only the restroom was placed in a separate room. All areas are well thought out to the smallest detail, so that every centimeter is optimally used; functionality, design, and operating efficiency are united here in close proximity. The slightly curved outer covering of the house is made of wood. In addition to a window which is similar to a giant bull's eye, an entire wall which is made completely of glass ensures generous light in the single room house. A somewhat different vision of living in the future.

Hier ist der Name Programm. Ein rotierendes Rondell bildet das Herzstück und Zentrum dieses bemerkenswerten Entwurfs von Luigi Colani. Der Designer, dessen Visitenkarte die organische Formensprache ist und dessen Entwürfe sich so bewusst von der Mehrheit der heute eher geradlinigen Architektur abheben, will dabei maximale Wohnfläche bei minimalem Außenmaß erzielen. Mit seiner Grundfläche von gerade einmal 6 auf 6 Metern spricht das Rotorhaus vor allem Singles und Kleinfamilien an. Im Kern des Colani-Rotorhauses sind 3 Funktionsbereiche – Schlafen, Küche und Bad – in einem Drehsystem vereint und können je nach Nutzungsbedarf durch Knopfdruck betreten werden. Einzig das WC wurde ausgegliedert und in einem separaten Raum untergebracht. Alle Bereiche sind bis ins kleinste Detail durchdacht, so dass jeder Zentimeter optimal genutzt wird; Funktionalität, Design und Wirtschaftlichkeit vereinen sich hier auf engstem Raum. Die leicht geschwungene Außenhülle des Gebäudes besteht aus Holz. Neben einem Fenster, das einem riesigen Bullauge gleicht, sorgt auch eine komplett verglaste Wand für großzügige Beleuchtung des Einraumwohnhauses. Eine etwas andere Vision vom Wohnen in der Zukunft.

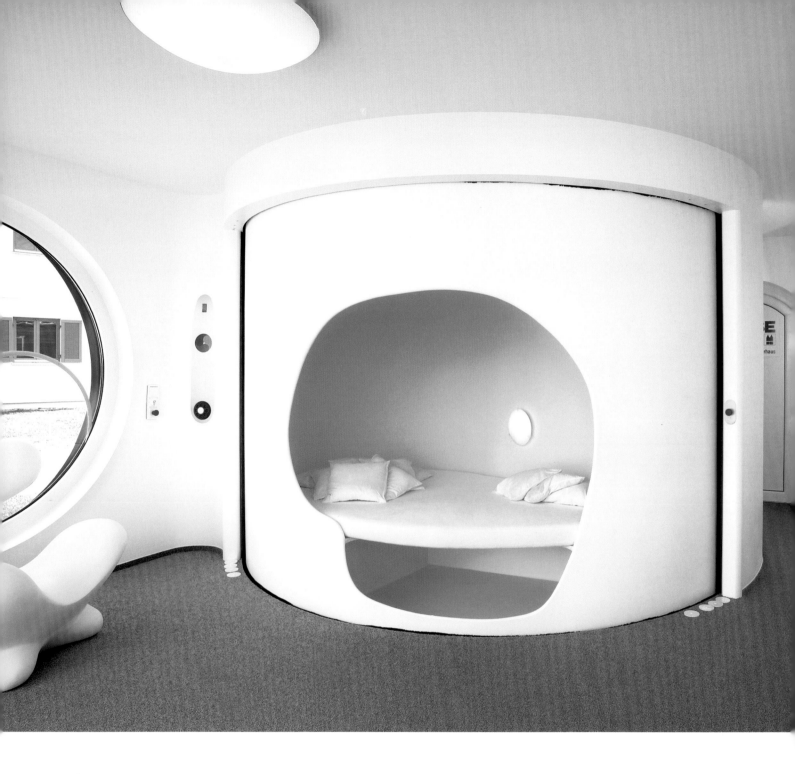

dockable dwelling | los angeles, ca . usa

DESIGN: Matias Creimer Studio

The conceptual scheme for the Dockable Dwelling project proposes a housing community derived from a space-age modular system. This strategy is paired with the camp aesthetics of American vernacular domestic building, namely the mobile home. Virtually completely factory-assembled, these units also made the freeway pilgrimage like their trailer park predecessors. But these houses are no longer migrant once joined together on site. Indeed initial delivery time directly affects the cost of prefab housing, so Creimer Studio sought to account for disparate industries, including transportation, to reduce cost. To do so, the architects adopted NASA's space station modular docking system, thereby reducing on-site labor. Instead mechanisation takes command by means of factory production in lieu of traditional building crafts. If efficiency determines the production and transportation of these units, it also characterizes their energy usage once inhabited. Equipped with Solar power systems, these houses are literally fueled with the extraterrestrial energy that figuratively propels their original design.

Der konzeptionelle Entwurf für die Dockable Dwellings sieht ein gemein-schaftliches Wohnwesen vor, das sich vom Baukastensystem des Welt-raumzeitalters ableitet. Diese Idee verbindet sich mit der Campingästhetik der landesüblichen amerikanischen Wohnhäuser, genauer gesagt dem transportablen Wohnmobil. Komplett in der Fabrik vorgefertigt, treten diese Wohnhäuser die klassische Pilgerfahrt auf dem Freeway an, ebenso wie ihre Vorgänger, die Wohnanhänger. Wenn sie allerdings am Bauplatz montiert sind, spricht man nicht länger von Nomadenhäusern. Da die Kosten auch von der Anlieferzeit der Fertigteilhäuser abhängig sind, wollten Creimer Studio unterschiedliche Industriezweige einbeziehen, einschließlich des Transportwesens, um die Häuser preislich günstig zu halten. Für die Umsetzung übernahmen die Architekten das Andockprinzip der Raumfahrt-stationen, wodurch sich der Arbeitsaufwand auf der Baustelle verringert. Statt des traditionellen Bauhandwerks steht nun die Technisierung durch die Fabrikproduktion im Vordergrund. Nicht nur Produktion und Transport sollten möglichst effizient sein, sondern auch der Energieverbrauch der bewohnten Häuser. Sie sind mit einem Solarenergiesystem ausgestattet und werden deshalb buchstäblich mit der überirdischen Energie versorgt, die auch ihr originelles Erscheinungsbild zu prägen scheint.

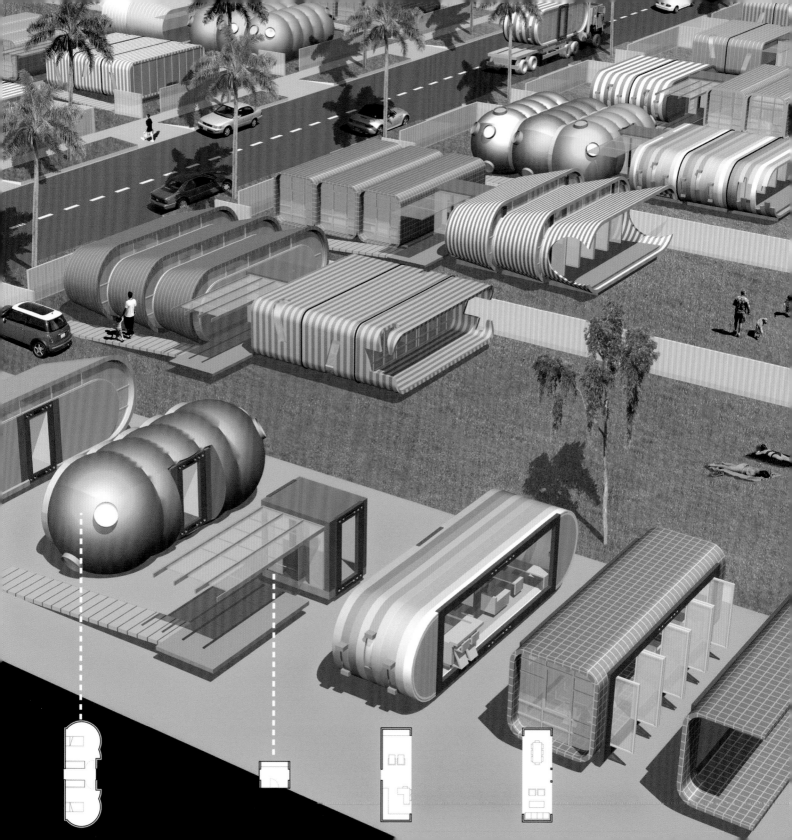

op den berg house | amersfoort . netherlands
DESIGN: Architectenbureau Jaco D. De Visser

The Op den Berg house is located within a larger community recently converted for residential use. Twenty of the seventy houses in the community were designated for customized construction including the Op den Berg house. Located on a small parcel of land, the home is compact, while managing to integrate the living area, kitchen, study, and bedrooms into a single spatial unity. Architect Jaco D. De Visser deployed illusionary elements to give the appearance of larger spaces. Therefore, the façade is intentionally skewed to compensate for the meagre site, while also causing the bedrooms to appear larger than they actually are. Windows throughout the steel and zinc façade also open up interior space with light, and moreover bring vistas of the garden and wooded surroundings to the interior. The house is further brought into dialogue with the nature through extensive timber construction in the rest of the home, a method of building that continually references the Dutch landscape.

Das Op den Berg House befindet sich in einer größeren Gemeinde, die erst kürzlich in ein Wohngebiet verwandelt wurde. Zwanzig der insgesamt 70 Häuser dieser Gemeinschaft waren für eine kundenspezifische Konstruktion bestimmt, einschließlich dem Op den Berg House. Das Haus liegt auf einer kleinen Parzelle und ist sehr kompakt in seinem Versuch, Wohnraum, Küche, Arbeitszimmer und Schlafräume in einer einzelnen räumlichen Einheit zusammenzufassen. Der Architekt Jaco D. De Visser nutzt optische Täuschungen, um die Räume größer wirken zu lassen. Außerdem wurde die Fassade gekrümmt, um die geringe Fläche des Bauplatzes zu kompensieren, was auch dazu führt, dass die Schlafräume größer erscheinen, als sie tatsächlich sind. Fenster innerhalb der Stahl- und Zinkfassade öffnen den Innenraum für das natürliche Licht und bringen gleichzeitig das Panorama des Gartens und der bewaldeten Umgebung ins Haus. Durch seine umfangreiche Holzkonstruktion im übrigen Teil des Gebäudes tritt es in einen Dialog mit der Natur; diese Bauweise nimmt immer wieder Bezug auf die niederländische Landschaft.

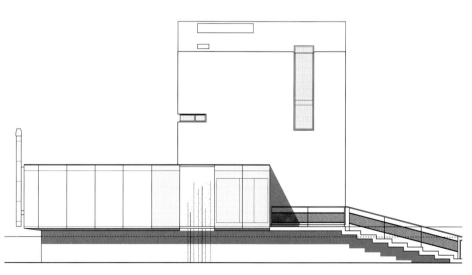

mobil chalet | munich . germany

DESIGN: DI Hans Georg Dieterle

A great amount of mobility, energy efficiency, good design and optimum functionality—Hans Georg Dieterle kept his promise to fulfill these requirements in a convincing manner with his patented solution for living and working. The mobile chalet can be used at various locations in an undisturbed natural setting as well as in the city thanks to its maneuverability by car or even by helicopter. Not only is the location variable but the usage as well, for example, as an atelier, office, vacation house, wellness center, or a guest house. A cleverly-designed solar power system, good insulation, and the best possible room volume make the house self-sufficient and therefore independent of its surroundings. The interior is similarly well thought out, which, with a floor space of 15 square meters, covers all the everyday areas. The shower, electric installations, and storage room disappear into a built-in closet which is as high as the room itself. Only a few movements are required and the dining area with table, which has two mobile sleeping areas, offers sleeping room for up to six people. Light-colored birch and maple, a folding door with large glass panes, and clear, angular lines give the 2 meter and 90 centimeter high room a light and friendly feeling. Materials such as stainless steel, glass, and wood ensure the absolute contemporary appearance of the cube and its size varies between 11 and 45 square meters, according to personal preference.

Höchste Mobilität, Energieeffizienz, gutes Design und optimale Funktionalität – diese Ansprüche löst Hans Georg Dieterle mit seiner patentierten Lösung für Wohnen & Arbeiten auf überzeugende Weise ein. Das Mobil Chalet ist dank seiner Manövrierfähigkeit mit Auto oder gar Hubschrauber an verschiedensten Standorten im Natur- und Stadtraum einsetzbar. Nicht nur der Standort ist variabel, sondern auch die Nutzung, beispielsweise als Atelier, Büro, Ferien-, Wellness- oder Gästehaus. Ein ausgeklügeltes Solarsystem, gute Dämmung und das optimierte Raumvolumen machen das Haus autark und damit unabhängig von der Umgebung. Ähnlich gut durchdacht ist der Innenraum, der mit einer Grundfläche von gerade einmal 15 Quadratmetern alle Alltagsbereiche abdeckt. In einem raumhohen Wandschrank verschwinden Dusche, Technik und Stauraum. Ein paar Handgriffe genügen und die Essecke mit Tisch bietet zusammen mit zwei schwenkbaren Schlafebenen für bis zu 6 Personen Schlafplätze. Helles Birken- und Ahornholz, eine großzügig verglaste Faltschiebetür und klare, kantige Linien lassen den 2,90 Meter hohen Raum hell und freundlich wirken. Materialien wie Edelstahl, Glas und Holz sorgen für ein absolut zeitgemäßes Erscheinungsbild des Kubus, dessen Größe je nach Wunsch zwischen 11 bis 45 Quadratmetern variiert.

casa minga | variable
DESIGN: Alejandro Dumay Claro

The designers of Casa Minga look to one key aspect of prefabricated housing, namely adaptability, to create a playful approach to the typology. The home is constructed quickly by factory production in three to four weeks. It is delivered by a truck to the site and positioned with a crane if required. Its design is based on a modular system comprising a horizontal unit that is exceptionally changeable. The home is low to the ground, therefore easily integrated into any landscape. Moreover, the uncomplicated volume ensures that it can be moved to a different site at the whim of the client. With the simplicity of its design, materials and even the use of the house are adaptable. Based on the client's needs, various elements, including windows, porches, and additional rooms, can be added. In the end, variability culminates in a synthesis to form both structural and design integrity.

Die Designer der Casa Minga nähern sich dem Thema vorgefertigter Häuser spielerisch an, indem sie sich vorrangig auf die Anpassungsfähigkeit dieses Häusertyps konzentrieren. Durch die industrielle Produktion kann das Haus in nur 3 bis 4 Wochen gebaut werden. Es wird mit einem Lastwagen zum Grundstück geliefert und nach Wunsch mit einem Kran aufgestellt. Das Design der Casa Minga basiert auf einem modularen System, das aus einer besonders leicht veränderbaren horizontalen Einheit besteht. Weil das Haus direkt auf dem Boden steht, fügt es sich gut in die Landschaft ein. Darüber hinaus garantiert seine unkomplizierte Größenordnung, dass es je nach Laune des Besitzers auf ein anderes Grundstück versetzt werden kann. Dank des einfachen Designs sind die Materialien und auch die Nutzungsform des Hauses anpassungsfähig. Je nach Bedarf der Bewohner können verschiedenste Bauteile, wie beispielsweise Fenster, Veranden und zusätzliche Räume, hinzugefügt werden. Letztendlich gipfelt die Variabilität in einer Synthese, die sowohl die strukturelle wie auch die gestalterische Integrität formt.

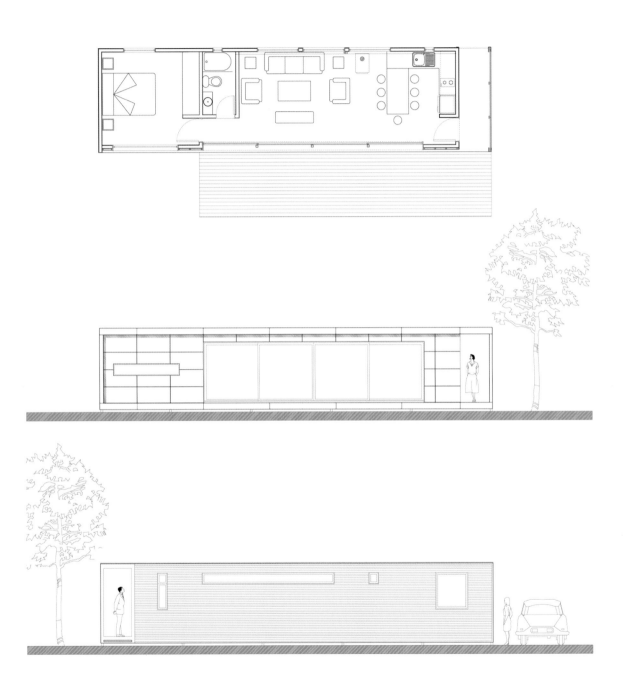

south hill park | london . uk
DESIGN: Robert Dye Associates

For an extension to an Edwardian semi-detached house, Robert Dye Associates conceived of two interlocking boxes. Though the black-stained cladding on the building's exterior provides a sensuous contrast to the environment, the extension is wholly integrated into the landscape. The simple geometries took their departure from the client's interest in Indian modernist architecture, which is notable for a unique reciprocity between interior and exterior. In doing so, the extension not only increases square footage, but also brings the home into a profound relationship with nature through light. A family room created on the ground floor flows into the exterior with a decked eating area. Sliding glass doors furnish an interior view of the garden, while further opening up the structure to light. Shadows from the garden's foliage project onto sandblasted windows in the master bathroom upstairs. Glass slits in both upstairs and downstairs cubes not only supply additional interior light, but also provide vistas across London. Timber-frame construction and sustainable materials intensify the building's organic quality and relationship with nature.

Als Anbau für ein Doppelhaus aus Englands Edwardianischer Zeit konzipierten Robert Dye Associates zwei ineinander greifende Kuben. Während die schwarz gefärbte Ummantelung der Gebäudehülle einen sinnlichen Kontrast zur Umgebung bildet, integriert sich der Erweiterungsbau vollkommen in das Landschaftsbild. Die schlichte Geometrie des Anbaus, die beachtenswert ist wegen der einzigartigen Wechselwirkung zwischen Innen- und Außenraum, geht auf das Interesse des Bauherren an moderner indischer Architektur zurück. Auf diese Weise wird durch den Anbau nicht nur Wohnfläche gewonnen, sondern das Licht lässt auch eine enge Verbindung zwischen dem Wohnhaus und der Natur entstehen. Im Erdgeschoss geht der Familienraum mit überdachtem Essbereich nahtlos in den Außenbereich über. Glasschiebetüren eröffnen Ausblicke aus dem Inneren in den Garten und sie lassen ebenso Licht herein. Das Laubwerk im Garten wirft Schatten auf die sandgestrahlten Fenster des Badezimmers im oberen Stockwerk. In beiden Stockwerken versorgen Glasöffnungen in den Kuben den Innenbereich nicht nur mit zusätzlichem Licht, sondern bieten auch Ausblicke quer über London. Die Holzbalkenkonstruktion und umweltverträgliche Materialien intensivieren die organische Qualität des Gebäudes und die Beziehung zur Natur.

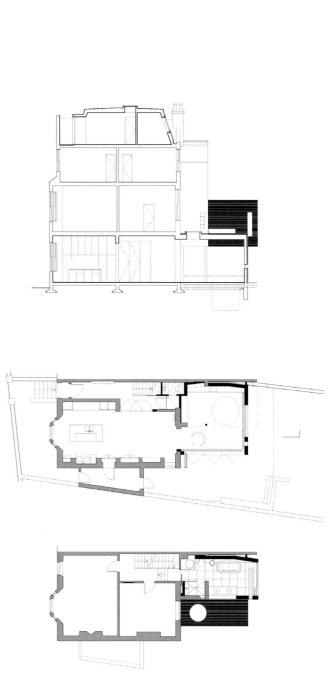

stealth house | london . uk
DESIGN: Robert Dye Associates

For the Stealth House, Robert Dye Associates was involved in designing a project financed and built by the client himself. A dramatic transformation of a bombsite in-fill house from the 1950s, the original structure was virtually demolished. With only a few original masonry elements left intact, the architect established the building's design intent and spatial qualities. A crucial aspect of the design was to maintain the house's integrity and relationship with the homes that line the street. To do so, grey-green felt forms an exterior roofscape extending up and over the penthouse to a cantilevered corner. In addition, stained-black timber was used to define the primary volume of the exterior. This cladding encloses the increased square footage of the home. To create continuity between interior and exterior, the cladding wraps around the contours of interior walls, and also creates unique vistas with interior windows and skylights. Minimally furnished, the inside of the house is defined by the sexy silhouettes of the building's exterior. Moreover, the dark finishes on the exterior offer lush contrast to airy and light filled interior spaces.

Beim Stealth House war das Architekturbüro Robert Dye Associates am Designprozess für ein Projekt beteiligt, das der Bauherr selbst finanzierte und baute. Bei der tief greifenden Verwandlung der Bebauung einer Baulücke aus den 50er Jahren des letzten Jahrhunderts wurde der ursprüngliche Bau nahezu komplett abgerissen. Nur wenige Teile des Mauerwerks blieben intakt und davon ausgehend entwickelte der Architekt die Design-Intentionen und die räumlichen Qualitäten des Gebäudes. Beim Design kam es vor allem darauf an, die Integrität des Gebäudes und das Verhältnis zu den anderen Häusern in der Straße zu wahren. Zu diesem Zweck wurde in ausladendem Winkel grüngrauer Filz über das Penthouse gespannt, der zudem einen äußeren Dachraum bildet. Zusätzlich wurde schwarz gebeiztes Holz dazu benutzt, das ursprüngliche Bauvolumen an der Fassade zu zeigen. Diese Ausführung kennzeichnet im Inneren die vergrößerte Wohnfläche. Um zwischen Innen- und Außenraum eine strukturelle Identität herzustellen, säumt die Verkleidung die Konturen der Innenwände und schafft mit Innenfenstern und Deckenlichtern ein einheitliches Bild. Mit seiner minimalistischen Einrichtung definiert sich das Innere des Wohnhauses klar durch die aufregenden Konturen des Gebäude-Äußeren. Darüber hinaus bietet das dunkle Finish außen einen großartigen Kontrast zum luftigen und lichtdurchfluteten Inneren.

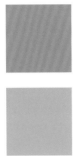

the flexible building system . haus ott | vorarlberg . austria

DESIGN: www.fuerrot.at, Simon Rümmele

The Austrian architects/developers, fuerrot, have developed "The Flexible Building System", in order to build as efficiently and inexpensively as possible. Some serially-produced building elements—from the pre-fabricated bathroom unit to the wooden element construction walls to the flexible balconies and stairs—offer the home builder the most amount freedom when designing the layout of the floor plan and with regard to the size. Haus Ott in the Austrian city of Schlins in Vorarlberg is one example of the most innovative prefabricated house in Europe, which was awarded the Energy Globe Award in 2003. The building system with quality of a "passive house" is characterized by its particular energy-efficiency, which is due in part to the excellent heat insulation of the walls and windows, as well as controllable ventilation system. The appearance of the flexible construction system depends on the owner, who can design it as individually as desired in the form and color. Depending on its design, the house can offer space for a variable number of inhabitants and can also be used for town houses and multi-story buildings. Under ideal circumstances, the construction period is only 10 days for immediate occupancy.

Um möglichst effizient und kostengünstig bauen zu können, haben die österreichischen Architektur-Entwickler fuerrot „Das flexible Bausystem" entworfen. Wenige seriell vorgefertigte Bauelemente – von der Fertignasszelle über Holzelement-Bauwände bis zu flexiblen Balkonen und Treppen – bieten dem Bauherren größtmögliche Freiheit bei der Grundrissgestaltung und hinsichtlich der Größe. Das Haus Ott im österreichischen Schlins in Vorarlberg ist dabei nur ein Beispiel für das innovativste Fertighaus Europas, das mit dem Energy Globe Award 2003 ausgezeichnet wurde. Das Bausystem mit Passivhausqualität zeichnet sich durch einen besonders sparsamen Energieverbrauch aus, der einer sehr guten Wärme-Isolierung von Wänden und Fenstern sowie kontrollierter Be- und Entlüftung zu verdanken ist. Das Erscheinungsbild des flexiblen Bausystems hängt von den Wünschen seines Besitzers ab, der es in Form und Farbigkeit individuell gestalten kann. Je nach Ausführung bietet es einer unterschiedlichen Anzahl von Bewohnern Platz und ist auch auf Reihen- und Mehrgeschossbauten anwendbar. Die Bauzeit bis zur schlüsselfertigen Übergabe beträgt im Idealfall nur 10 Tage.

summerhouse | hálsasveit, borgarfjörður . iceland

DESIGN: Gláma Kim Arkitektar, Ólafur Mathiesen

Nestled in the sparse, yet breathtaking landscape of Iceland, the Summerhouse in Hálsasveit has the special added benefit of the unique views which open up in all directions. To the south, the landscape slopes slightly and a small river winds its way through the countryside. The domicile was erected at its current location between 1999 and 2002 in a total of three phases of construction. The largest portion of the construction was delivered pre-manufactured, the smaller bedroom wing were fabricated off-site in the winter and assembled on-site in the spring. All main living spaces are located in the main building: on the west end are an open kitchen, bathrooms, living and dining area, as well as the entry. A terrace adjoins the living area. The architect, Ólafur Mathiesen from the office of Glama Kim Arkitektar enclosed the wood frame construction of the Summerhouse in a corrugated metal cladding; the interior is however completely cladded with birch plywood. Cork was selected for the floors. The construction was carried out simply and precisely and in this manner reflects the clarity and beauty of the environment. The third workstep of construction are the exterior living areas, terraces, outdoor shower and a small pool.

Eingebettet in die karge, atemberaubende Landschaft Islands, lebt das Summerhouse in Hálsasveit besonders von den einzigartigen Ausblicken, die sich hier in alle Himmelsrichtungen eröffnen. Nach Süden hin ist das Gelände leicht abfallend und durch die Landschaft schlängelt sich hier ein kleiner Fluss. Zwischen 1999 und 2002 entstand das Domizil an seinem heutigen Standort in insgesamt 3 Bauphasen. Der größere Teil der Konstruktion wird vorgefertigt angeliefert, der kleinere Gebäuderiegel mit Schlafeinheit wird im Winter vorproduziert und anschließend auf dem Bauplatz im Frühjahr errichtet. Im Hauptgebäude befinden sich alle Gemeinschaftsräume: eine offene Küche, Bad, Wohn- und Essbereich, WC sowie der Eingang am Westende. Eine Terrasse schließt direkt an den Wohnraum an. Der Architekt Ólafur Mathiesen von Glama Kim Arkitektar fasst die Holzrahmenkonstruktion des Summerhouse im Außenbereich mit einer gewellten Metallschalung ein, der Innenbereich ist dagegen komplett mit Schalungsplatten aus Birkenholz verkleidet. Für den Fußboden wurde Kork gewählt. Die Konstruktion ist einfach und präzise ausgeführt und spiegelt die Klarheit und Schönheit der Umgebung wider. In der dritten Bauphase kommt ein äußerer Wohnbereich, Terrassen, eine im Freien befindliche Dusche und ein kleiner Pool hinzu.

cocobello | variable

DESIGN: Peter Haimerl

Showroom, office, press box, or artist's atelier—there are almost no restrictions to the variety of uses of the container module, Cocobello. The prototype which was presented for the first time at the biennale architecture exhibition in 2003 is a vision of the architect, Peter Haimerl, and defines the term mobility in a completely new way. "You pack your bags and take them with you. Do the same with your living space," suggests the architect. The building is made of three building segments bolted together and can be extended horizontally as well as vertically. It reminds you a little of something from outer space. Thus, a two story atelier room can be constructed in only two steps in which the shelves are automatically extended. During transportation, all the essential elements of the container module remain inside—therefore eliminating moving out, moving back in and rearranging. The façade of the steel frame construction, which is covered with aluminum, can be created in any desired color and can fulfill various functions; such as a "shop window", plane of projection, or as an exhibition space. These characteristics and the extremely simple transportation from A to B make the "Omni Box" an especially interesting space used on a temporary basis such as on the edge of a city or on fallow land, but also as a display downtown.

Showroom, Arbeitsplatz, Pressekabine oder Künstleratelier – der Nutzungsvielfalt des Container-Moduls Cocobello sind fast keine Grenzen gesetzt. Dieser erstmalig auf der Architekturbiennale 2003 präsentierte Prototyp ist eine Vision des Architekten Peter Haimerl und definiert den Begriff Mobilität auf völlig neue Weise. „Sie packen Ihre Tasche und nehmen sie überall mit. Machen Sie das Gleiche mit Ihrem Raum", schlägt der Architekt vor. Ein bisschen wie von einem anderen Stern wirkt dabei das Gebilde aus drei ineinander verschränkten Bauteilen, die man sowohl horizontal als auch vertikal auseinander fahren kann. So entsteht in nur zwei Schritten ein zweigeschossiger Atelierraum, in dem die Regale automatisch ausgefahren werden. Beim Transport bleiben alle wesentlichen Elemente des Container-Moduls im Inneren – so entfällt das Ein-, Aus- und Umräumen. Die Fassade der mit Aluminium beplankten Stahlrahmenkonstruktion wird farblich nach Wunsch gestaltet und kann verschiedene Funktionen erfüllen: Schaufenster, Projektionsebene oder Ausstellungsfläche. Diese Eigenschaften und ein extrem einfacher Transport von A nach B machen die Omni-Box besonders interessant für zeitlich begrenzte Nutzungsflächen wie etwa städtische Randzonen oder Brachland, aber auch im Zentrum als Display.

wunschhaus #1 | hamburg-sülldorf . germany

DESIGN: heide von beckerath alberts architekten

"The German Dream House" was the motto of a contest which the magazine, "Stern", held together with the savings and loan association, "Schwäbisch Hall". The architects Tim Heide, Verena von Beckerath and Andrew Alberts submitted their own personal wunschhaus#1, which was later developed for serial production. The construction was realized for the first time in a settlement for show houses in Hamburg-Sülldorf. The architects´ goal was to unite different and above all changing ways of life under one roof. The respective definition of the rooms is the inhabitants´ choice, which they may use as they like. The wunschhaus#1 offers not only open but also enclosed rooms, in which sliding doors in the inside lend themselves to this flexibility. This single family house is impressive with its clear and plain structure. Large sliding glass doors leading to the outside and the flexible floor plan design benefit light, spacious living.

„Das Wunschhaus der Deutschen", so lautete das Thema eines Wettbewerbs, den die Zeitschrift Stern gemeinsam mit der Bausparkasse Schwäbisch Hall ausschrieb. Die Architekten Tim Heide, Verena von Beckerath and Andrew Alberts reichten ihr ganz persönliches wunschhaus#1 ein, das später für die serielle Produktion weiterentwickelt wurde. Im Rahmen einer Musterhaussiedlung in Hamburg-Sülldorf wurde der Bau zum ersten Mal realisiert. Ziel der Architekten war es, verschiedene und vor allen Dingen sich verändernde Lebensgewohnheiten unter einem Dach zu vereinen. Die jeweilige Definition der Räume bleibt den Bewohnern überlassen, die sie je nach Wunsch nutzen können. Das wunschhaus#1 bietet sowohl offene als auch geschlossene Räume, wobei Schiebetüren im Inneren diese Flexibilität unterstützen. Das Einfamilienhaus überzeugt durch eine klare und schnörkellose Struktur. Großformatige außenlaufende Schiebefenstertüren und der offen gehaltene Grundriss begünstigen helles, großzügiges Wohnen.

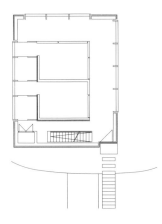

haus alsterblick | hamburg . germany

DESIGN: Tim Heide

The extension of the Haus Alsterblick in Hamburg was created to be autonomous and flexible in its usage. Furthermore, it was supposed to function independently of the single family home built in the 1950's as well as be adaptable with regard to the home builder's various usage possibilities (as a living space or an atelier). The expansion was planned so that two generations could communicate with one another and still lead a "peaceful coexistence". The architecture of both areas is vastly different. The subject of "old/new" also played an important role during the structural realization: traditional craftsmanship techniques cooperating with modern manufacturing methods. Based on a "balloon framing system", six large, pre-fabricated segments were constructed on site. A light-weight clay wall was put on the multi-layered exterior wall. Clay has favorable characteristics on the room's climate and ensures a pleasant atmosphere in the interior. Furthermore, the exterior covering of the house and the supply cube in the interior are independent of each other.

Autonom und flexibel in der Nutzung sollte die Erweiterung von Haus Alsterblick in Hamburg sein. Und sie sollte unabhängig vom Einfamilienhaus aus den fünfziger Jahren funktionieren sowie anpassungsfähig sein im Hinblick auf unterschiedliche Nutzungsmöglichkeiten durch den Bauherren (Wohnraum, Atelier). Die Erweiterung ist so konzipiert, dass zwei Generationen in einem Dialog stehen und nebeneinander eine „friedliche Koexistenz" führen können. Die Architektur der beiden Bereiche setzt sich dabei stark voneinander ab. Auch bei der baulichen Umsetzung spielt die Thematik Alt/Neu eine wichtige Rolle: Traditionelle Handwerkstechniken kooperieren mit modernen Fertigungsmethoden. Basierend auf einem Balloon-Framing-System werden 6 vorgefertigte Großtafeln vor Ort aufgebaut. Der mehrschichtigen Außenwand wird innen eine Leichtlehmwand aufgesetzt. Die guten raumklimatischen Eigenschaften des Lehms sorgen für eine angenehme Atmosphäre im Innenraum. Dabei sind die äußere Hülle des Gebäudes und der Versorgungskubus im Inneren voneinander unabhängig.

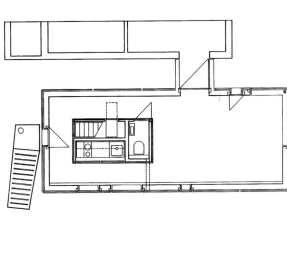

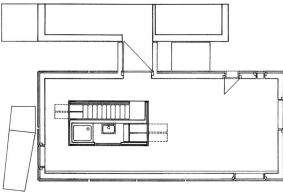

'touch' house | helsinki . finland
DESIGN: Heikkinen-Komonen Architects

In 2000, Heikkinen-Komonen Architects, from Finland, presented this prototype of the serially-produced single family home at the home exposition in Tuusula, Finland. The goal of this design was to develop an industrially pre-fabricated house for a family of four. Although living space in the city is calculated rather scarcely, it was supposed to be suitable to be built in a city and to provide sufficient space for each of the inhabitants. While the exterior of the pre-fabricated house is clearly outlined, the interior is very interesting because of the various sizes, the partitioning and height of the rooms. The roof, which from a bird's eye view has the form of a square envelope, is made of glass shingles above the veranda, gallery from the bedroom and sauna terrace. Thus these areas are sufficiently and generously provided with daylight. The center of the building is a one and one-half story high open space with a kitchen island, which includes the living room, dining room and cooking area. Through their arrangement, the various zones are also defined and differentiated.

Das finnische Architekturbüro Heikkinen-Komonen Architects präsentierte im Jahr 2000 auf der Wohnhaus-Ausstellung in Tuusula, Finnland, den Prototyp des in Serie produzierbaren Einfamilienhauses. Ziel des Entwurfs war es, ein industriell vorgefertigtes Haus für eine vierköpfige Familie zu entwickeln. Obwohl Wohnraum in der Stadt knapp bemessen ist, sollte es für eine städtische Bebauung geeignet sein und dabei ausreichend Raum für jeden Bewohner zur Verfügung stellen. Während das Äußere des Fertighauses klar umrissen ist, lebt der Innenraum von der Spannung, die durch unterschiedliche Größe, Aufteilung und Raumhöhe der Raumvolumina entsteht. Das Dach, das aus der Vogelperspektive die Form eines viereckigen Briefumschlages hat, besteht über Veranda, Schlafgalerie und Saunaterrasse aus Glasschindeln. So werden diese Bereiche ausreichend und großzügig mit Tageslicht versorgt. Das Zentrum des Gebäudes bildet ein eineinhalb Stockwerke hoher Luftraum mit einer Kücheninsel, die Wohn-, Ess- und Kochbereich mit einbezieht. Auch durch die Einrichtung werden die einzelnen Zonen definiert und voneinander abgesetzt.

holzkuben zum wohnen und arbeiten | wolfurt . austria
DESIGN: k_m architektur

An open slat-like casing made of indigenous silver fir dominates the mostly closed façade of the Boehler house on the northern side. To the south, the house opens itself up even more. The two horizontal and vertical parts of the structure overlapping into one another with their interplay of openings and cuts make the exterior into the interior and vice-versa. The office is located on the ground level with its own entrance and integrated parking space, whereas the living and sleeping areas are found on the first and second floors. There are also terraces facing the east, south, and west. A flexible floor plan design is made possible by the large spans and cantilever of the wood frame construction. Thanks to the large pre-fabricated wood construction elements, the single family home for 4 to 5 persons was able to be built in only 4 days. The consistent pattern of simple, well-planned construction kept the production costs comparatively low and, on the other hand, enabled the home builder to do a large portion of do-it-yourself work, which had an overall positive effect on the total costs. No synthetic wood preservatives and paints were used for the entire construction due to health and ecological concerns. The property lies on agricultural land which ensures an unspoiled view from every floor.

Eine offene lamellenartige Schalung aus heimischer Weißtanne dominiert die eher geschlossene Fassade des Wohnhauses Boehler auf der Nordseite. Nach Süden hin öffnet sich das Haus dafür umso mehr. Die beiden horizontal und vertikal ineinander übergreifenden Baukörper machen mit ihrem Wechselspiel aus Öffnungen und Einschnitten den Außenraum zum Innenraum und umgekehrt. Das Büro befindet sich mit eigenem Zugang und integriertem Autoabstellplatz im Erdgeschoss, während sich die Wohn- und Schlafbereiche auf das erste und zweite Obergeschoss verteilen. Hier befinden sich auch die nach Osten, Süden und Westen gerichteten Terrassen. Große Spannweiten und Auskragungen des Holzrahmenbaus ermöglichen eine flexible Grundrisseinteilung. Dank großer, vorgefertigter Holzbauelemente konnte das Einfamilienhaus für 4 bis 5 Personen in nur 4 Tagen aufgebaut werden. Das konsequente Raster der einfachen, durchdachten Konstruktion hielt die Herstellungskosten vergleichsweise niedrig und ermöglichte andererseits einen hohen Anteil an Eigenleistung seitens der Bauherren, was sich wiederum positiv auf die Gesamtkosten auswirkte. Am gesamten Bau wurde aus gesundheitlichen und ökologischen Gründen auf synthetische Holzschutzmittel und Lacke verzichtet. Das Grundstück liegt auf einer landwirtschaftlichen Nutzfläche, die den unverbaubaren Blick in jedem Stockwerk sicherstellt.

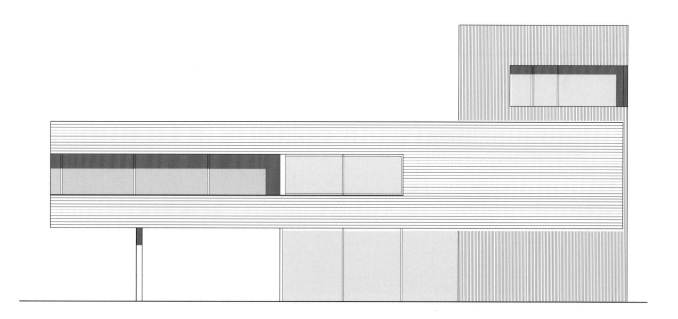

wohnen mit der natur | bregenz . austria

DESIGN: k_m architektur

The location alone of this single family home in Bregenz, with a clear view of Lake Constance is unique. The property which is located on the slope of a proverbial green meadow offered the optimum conditions for the office of k_m.architektur to realize the design which captivates through its clear, symmetrical form and the use of natural materials. While the ground floor of concrete builds a solid foundation, the upper part of the building was constructed in a wood element structure. A loggia which encircles the building on the "water side" fulfills the home builder's desire for an open living space. This loggia connects all the rooms on the upper floors and creates a flowing transition between interior and exterior. The effect is intensified by sliding glass doors as high as the room itself on this side of the façade. The back of the house appears to be more closed, though a small set of outside stairs enables direct contact to nature at any time. A straight set of stairs in the middle of the landscaped courtyard serves as an open entrance area to the building. The outer skin made of wood encloses the diverse openings and views and keeps the building optically together despite its interplay of open space and interior space. The floating character of the parts of the structure results from the concrete segments that are placed slightly offset on which the building rests.

Allein schon die Lage dieses Einfamilienhauses in Bregenz mit freiem Blick auf den Bodensee ist einmalig. Ein Hanggrundstück auf der sprichwörtlich grünen Wiese bot optimale Voraussetzungen für das Büro k_m.architektur, um einen Entwurf zu realisieren, der durch seine klare, symmetrische Form und die Verwendung naturbelassener Materialien besticht. Während das Erdgeschoss aus Beton eine solide Basis bildet, wurde der obere Teil des Gebäudes in einer Holzelement-Bauweise errichtet. Eine umlaufende Loggia auf der „Wasserseite" erfüllt den Wunsch der Bauherren nach einer offenen Wohnform. Diese Loggia verbindet alle Räume im Obergeschoss und schafft einen fließenden Übergang zwischen Außen- und Innenraum. Verstärkt wird diese Wirkung durch raumhohe Schiebeglastüren auf dieser Seite der Fassade. Die Rückseite des Hauses wirkt eher verschlossen, doch eine kleine Außentreppe ermöglicht jederzeit den direkten Kontakt zur Natur. Als offener Zugangsbereich zum Gebäude dient eine einläufige Treppe im mittig angelegten Innenhof. Die Außenhaut aus Holz umschließt die verschiedenen Öffnungen und Durchblicke und hält das Gebäude trotz des Wechselspiels aus Frei- und Innenräumen optisch zusammen. Der schwebende Charakter des Baukörpers entsteht durch die leicht nach hinten versetzten Betonscheiben, auf denen das Gebäude ruht.

wohnen am waldrand | lindau . germany

DESIGN: k_m architektur

For the design by the architects, k_m.architektur, a concrete segment, which is as high as the house, shields the building to the edge of the forest and at the same time creates interesting views of the nearby glade. On the south side, a glass façade stretches the length of the house and directly faces the garden, which is in this manner optically integrated into the house. The exterior is then the interior and the interior is the exterior. On the ground floor, there are smaller storage rooms, a work area and even a sauna. The top floor is divided into common rooms which are located in offset floating frames and the individual rooms are found in the back of the protected part of the wooden cube. A tool shed, also part of the house, will be optically integrated by use of the concrete segment mentioned and allows interesting spaces to be created. The building was planned in the wood-element style of construction. Through the surrounding frame and the slightly offset ground floor, the upper floor has a floating character. A large portion of the elements for the energy-efficient house is produced in the manufacturing plant, which helps to eliminate delays due to bad weather or other factors on the construction site.

Bei diesem Entwurf der Architekten k_m.architektur schirmt eine haushohe Betonscheibe das Gebäude zum Waldrand hin ab und inszeniert gleichzeitig Ausblicke auf die nahe gelegene Lichtung. Auf der Südseite erstreckt sich eine Glasfassade über die gesamte Länge und grenzt direkt an den Garten, der auf diese Weise optisch in das Gebäude eingebunden wird. Der Außenraum wird so zum Innenraum, der Innenraum zum Außenraum. Im Erdgeschoss sind die Nebenräume, ein Arbeitsbereich und eine Sauna untergebracht. Das Obergeschoss gliedert sich in die Gemeinschaftsräume, die sich im vorgesetzten, schwebenden Bügel befinden, und in die Individualräume im hinteren, geschützten Teil des Holzkubus. Eine ebenfalls zum Gebäude gehörende Gerätebox wird optisch durch die erwähnte Betonscheibe einbezogen und lässt interessante Zwischenräume entstehen. Das Gebäude wurde in Holzelement-Bauweise geplant. Durch den einfassenden Bügel und das etwas zurückgesetzte Erdgeschoss erhält das obere Stockwerk einen schwebenden Charakter. Ein Großteil der Elemente für das Niedrigenergiehaus wird in der Werkstatt vorgefertigt, wodurch eine Standzeit wegen Schlechtwetter oder anderer Einflüsse auf der Baustelle vermieden wird.

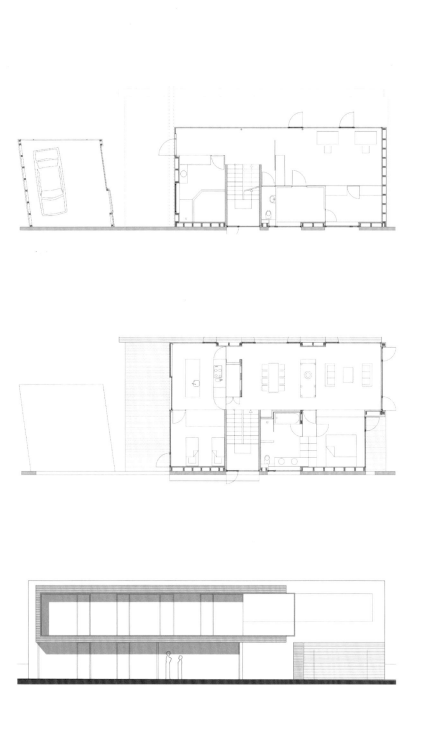

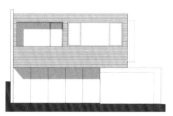

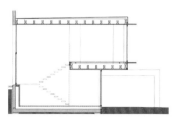

UP!house 1500

DESIGN: konyk

The UP!house is a refined version of a prefabricated house commissioned previously by Dwell magazine. konyk looked to the automotive industry for key analogies in the project's design. Fabricated in China and imported to the United Stated, the client can choose from a range of options, including power windows and home theater entertainment packages, as if customizing a new car. With its factory produced lightweight steel tube construction, architect Craig Konyk likens the house's frame to an automobile "chassis". The house's walls, or "body" (another of the architect's references to car culture) is comprised of high gloss coated metal panels with matching tinted glass. On the interior, bright white epoxy coated panels create an airy streamlined appearance. But this house is not only prefabricated. Its parts can be reassembled, allowing clients to add of remove parts of the house as their needs change. The house can even be disassembled and reassembled on a new plot of land. With this house, you can take it with you!

Das UP!house ist die verfeinerte Version eines Fertigteilhauses, das erst kürzlich von der Zeitschrift Dwell in Auftrag gegeben wurde. Das Architekturbüro konyk orientierte sich beim Design dieses Projektes an Analogien aus der Fahrzeugindustrie. Erst in China hergestellt, dann in die USA geliefert, kann der Kunde aus einer breiten Palette von Möglichkeiten wählen, einschließlich automatischer Fenster und Heimkino-Angebotspakete, als ob man einen neuen Wagen ausstatten würde. Mit der vorgefertigten leichten Stahlröhrenkonstruktion passt der Architekt Craig Konyk das Gerüst des Hauses an das Fahrgestell eines Automobils an. Die Wände des Hauses oder sein „Körper" (eine weitere Referenz des Architekten an den Autokult) bestehen aus Hochglanz-Metallplatten mit farblich angepasstem Glas. Im Inneren lassen helle weiße mit Epoxid beschichtete Paneele ein luftiges, stromlinienförmiges Erscheinungsbild entstehen. Aber dieses Haus ist nicht nur vorgefertigt, seine Teile können auch wieder neu zusammengesetzt werden. Das ermöglicht es dem Besitzer, Gebäudeteile hinzuzufügen oder zu entfernen, je nach Bedarf. Das Haus kann sogar komplett abgebaut und auf einem anderen Grundstück wieder errichtet werden. Dieses Haus kann man überall mit hinnehmen!

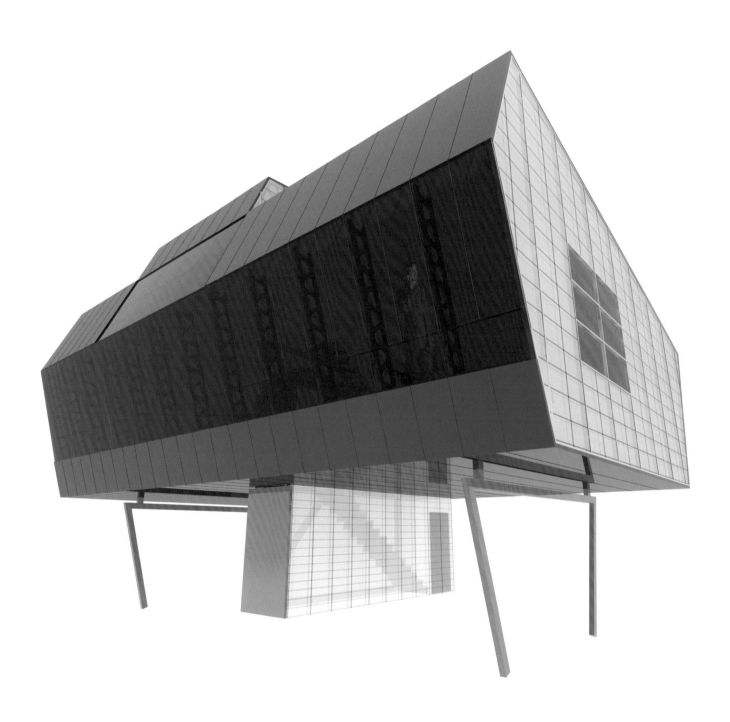

house 4 two | illingen . germany
D E S I G N : Frederik Künzel mit De Fries Architekturbüro

As the name suggests, the house in Illingen, Germany was planned for two people. It was not supposed to be a pre-fabricated house, however, just as affordable. The builders of the home, Kerstin Endres and Michael Lang, wanted to include their own individual ideas and have the greatest amount of flexibility with regard to the design of the interior. The architect, Frederik Künzel, developed his design on this basis. According to the groove and tongue principle, the pre-fabricated, two-story exterior walls are put onto the wood frame construction. The foundation is made of a steel-fiber cement slab. The shell elements remain visible in the interior, whereas all of the installations disappear in the floor or in the non-bearing interior walls. The floor is made only of sealed concrete, which was intentionally left so. The flexible floor plan allows the inhabitants to make changes afterwards according to personal preferences. In addition, the ventilated flat roof made of simple, pre-fabricated building segments was planned so that the future owners could make their own personal changes. The standard size of the building segments, unconventional materials, and a large do-it-yourself portion on the part of the home builders keep the price per square extremely low price.

Wie der Name schon verrät, wurde das Haus in Illingen, Deutschland, für 2 Personen konzipiert. Kein Fertighaus sollte es sein und doch genauso günstig. Die Bauherren Kerstin Endres und Michael Lang wollten ihre individuellen Wünsche einbringen und einen möglichst großen Spielraum bei der Gestaltung des Innenraumes haben. Auf dieser Basis entwickelte der Architekt Frederik Künzel seinen Entwurf. Dabei werden nach dem Nut- und Federprinzip zusammengesetzte zweigeschossige Außenwände auf einer Holzrahmenkonstruktion angebracht. Das Fundament bildet eine Stahlfaser-Betonplatte. Die Rohbauelemente bleiben im Inneren sichtbar, während alle Installationen im Fußboden oder in den nicht tragenden Innenwänden verschwinden. Auf einen Bodenbelag wurde bewusst verzichtet, der Fußboden besteht aus versiegeltem Estrich. Der flexible Grundriss ermöglicht den Bewohnern je nach Wunsch und Bedarf nachträgliche Änderungen. Auch das Kaltdach aus Nagelplattenbindern ist so konzipiert, dass der zukünftige Besitzer selbst Hand anlegen konnte. Die genormte Größe der Bauteile, unkonventionelle Materialien und ein hoher Anteil an Eigeninitiative seitens der Bauherren ermöglichten einen extrem niedrigen Quadratmeterpreis.

m-house | variable
DESIGN: Mae Architects and Tim Pyne

The appearance of the m-house—pronounced "mouse"—strongly reminds one of a trailer with its dimensions of an oversized camper. Each of the two modules measures 3 meters in width (the maximum width permitted in traffic) and 17 meters in length. Only one day is required to build the pre-fabricated segments on the site. After installation, the m-house is ready for immediate occupancy. The owner can decide whether he/she would like to keep the domicile as simple as possible in the furnishings in the "back to nature" category or whether he/she would like to have everything completely built for him/her into a residential building. Michael Howe, partner at Mae Architects, paid careful attention that all the building regulations were adhered to, and thus the trailer meets all the specifications of a normal house. The m-house has already gained worldwide attention in the press, because it is a prime example of a successful combination of efficiency and design. High-quality building materials, optimum insulation, and quality workmanship of the materials such as wood, aluminum, and glass guarantee the longevity of the m-house. It is then irrelevant whether the m-house is used as a temporary country estate in the middle of a green meadow or as an additional living space in a inner courtyard in the city. The "mouse" is flexible in the interior as well, according to the function and needs of the user.

Mit den Ausmaßen eines überdimensionierten Wohnanhängers erinnert das m-house – ausgesprochen „Maus" – auch optisch stark an das Erscheinungsbild eines Caravans. Jedes der beiden Module misst 3 Meter in der Breite (angelehnt an die maximal erlaubte Breite im Straßenverkehr) und 17 Meter in der Länge. Nur ein Tag wird benötigt, um die beiden fabrikfertigen Teile vor Ort aufzubauen. Nach der Installation ist das m-house sofort bezugsbereit. Der Besitzer kann entscheiden, ob er das Domizil in der Kategorie „zurück zur Natur" möglichst einfach in der Ausstattung halten möchte oder den kompletten Ausbau zum Wohnhaus wünscht. Michael Howe von Mae Architects achtete genauestens darauf, dass die Bauvorschriften eingehalten wurden, und so erfüllt der Caravan alle Auflagen eines normalen Hauses. In der Presse hat das m-house bereits weltweite Aufmerksamkeit erregt, weil es ein ideales Beispiel für die gelungene Verbindung von Wirtschaftlichkeit und gutem Design ist. Qualitativ hochwertige Bauteile, optimale Dämmung und sauber verarbeitete Materialien wie Holz, Aluminium und Glas garantieren für eine lange Lebensdauer. Dabei ist es nebensächlich, ob das m-house als temporärer Landsitz mitten auf der grünen Wiese oder als Wohnraumergänzung in der Stadt im Hinterhof genutzt wird. Flexibel ist die „Maus" auch im Innenbereich, je nach Funktion und Wünschen des Nutzers.

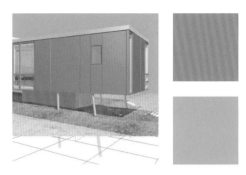

modulome | san francisco, ca . usa

DESIGN: Nottoscale / Peter Strzebniok & Matthias Troitzsch

When the architects, Peter Strzebniok and Matthias Troitzsch from Nottoscale, found out that only 4 percent of homes in the USA are designed by architects, they wondered why that was the case. During their research, they learned that it is a common misconception that good architects are not affordable; they are more or less a luxury. The architects themselves are another reason why many home builders avoid the architectural scene. Many architects would rather design one unique home than be creative for the general public. The architects from Nottoscale set upon these points with their concept of the Modulome, for which they used marketing and production ideas from the automobile industry. Modulome is a modular construction system with pre-fabricated, mass-produced building elements. The basic unit is a relatively simple yet expandable module. The grid or heart of the building is a steel framework which allows individual building elements to be interchanged. Individualized requests can therefore be taken into account. Modulome can be used for various types of houses; whether it is a free-standing single family home, with a courtyard, as a duplex or a high-rise apartment house—because the ability to offer living space for different ways of life is a further advantage of this concept. The team of architects from California has come a great deal closer to the goal of offering quality design at an affordable price.

Als die Architekten Peter Strzebniok und Matthias Troitzsch von Nottoscale herausfanden, dass nur 4 Prozent der Häuser in den USA aus Architektenhand kommen, fragten sie sich, warum das so ist. Bei ihren Recherchen stießen sie auf den weit verbreiteten Irrglauben, dass gute Architektur nicht erschwinglich, sondern ein Luxus sei. Ein anderer Grund, warum viele Bauherren die Architekturszene meiden, sind Architekten selbst. Oft entwerfen sie lieber ein Unikat als für die breite Masse kreativ zu werden. An diesen beiden Punkten setzen die Architekten mit ihrem Konzept des Modulome an, für das sie Marketing- und Produktionsideen aus der Automobilindustrie nutzen. Modulome ist ein Baukastensystem mit vorgefertigten, in Masse produzierten Bauteilen. Die Grundeinheit ist ein verhältnismäßig einfaches, aber ausbaufähiges Modul. Das Raster und Herzstück des Gebäudes, ein Stahlgerippe, erlaubt den Austausch einzelner Bauteile. Dadurch können auch individuelle Wünsche berücksichtigt werden. Modulome ist für verschiedene Haustypen anwendbar, ob nun frei stehend, mit Innenhof, als Doppelhaushälfte oder als mehrstöckiges Wohnhaus – denn Wohnraum für verschiedene Lebensformen zu bieten, das ist ein weiterer Anspruch dieses Konzepts. Das Architektenteam aus Kalifornien ist damit dem Ziel, gutes Design zu einem erschwinglichen Preis anzubieten, ein großes Stück näher gekommen.

portable house | venice, ca . usa

DESIGN: Office of Mobile Design (OMD) / Jennifer Siegal

The Portable House reconstitutes the primitive migrant dwelling for the global nomad. Whereas prehistoric man settled in makeshift habitats constructed from ingenuous elements, this contemporary conception engages materials and production methods only made available with the technological revolution. Like its ancient predecessor, however, the Portable House adapts, relocates, and reorients itself to changing social and physical environments. With its changeable dimensions, the structure both expands and contracts. Sustainable materials ensure the longevity of the structure. Since it is also portable, parts of the house adjust to accommodate natural light and airflow in different climates. Its social function is also adaptable when individual houses are grouped together, as the Office of Mobile Design has proposed for Ecoville. Once made part of a community, multiple units can be integrated with common extensions of the dwellings including gardens, courtyards, and side yards. Indeed the Portable House exemplifies its potential as an alternative to such traditional forms of mobile housing as trailer homes. It is completely factory assembled, and is delivered to the site ready to install.

Das Portable House greift die einfache Wanderbehausung für den globalen Nomaden wieder auf. Während der vorgeschichtliche Mensch in Behelfsunterkünften aus einfachsten Bauteilen lebte, nutzt diese moderne Variante Materialien und Produktionsmethoden, die der technische Fortschritt erst ermöglicht hat. Doch wie seine Vorgänger passt sich das Portable House an seine jeweilige wechselnde soziale und physische Umgebung an, es stellt sich darauf ein und orientiert sich an ihr. Dank seiner veränderbaren Dimensionen kann die Konstruktion erweitert oder verkleinert werden, wobei robuste Materialien die Langlebigkeit gewährleisten. Da es mobil ist, können Teile des Hauses an das natürliche Licht und die Luftzirkulation in verschiedenen Klimazonen angepasst werden. Auch seine soziale Funktion ist anpassungsfähig, denn ähnlich wie beim Entwurf Ecoville des Büros für Mobiles Design können die einzelnen Gebäude in Gruppen zusammengefasst werden. Ist aus mehreren Häusern eine solche Gemeinschaft entstanden, können die einzelnen Einheiten durch Gemeinschaftsflächen wie Gärten, Hinter- und Seitenhöfe zusammengefasst werden. Tatsächlich stellt das Portable House eine mögliche Alternative zu den traditionellen Formen der mobilen Behausung, wie etwa Wohnwägen, dar. Die in der Fabrik komplett vorproduzierten Teile werden zur schnellen Montage an den Bauplatz geliefert.

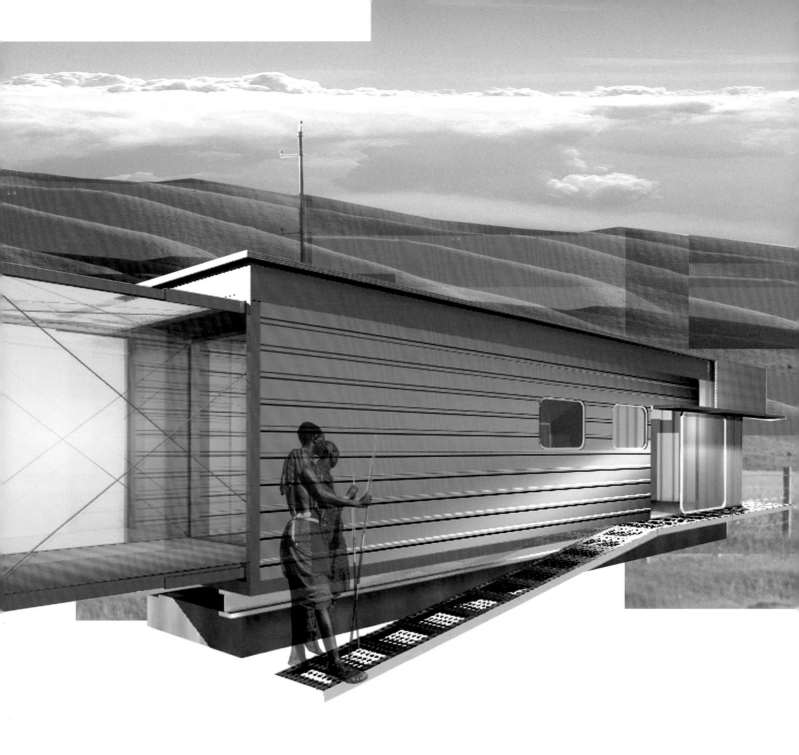

ecoville | variable

D E S I G N : Office of Mobile Design (OMD) / Jennifer Siegal

Ecoville, based on Office of Mobile Design's Portable House project provides low-cost living and studio space for Artists-in-Residence in downtown Los Angeles's burgeoning artists' community. Composed of modular units, their standardization does not mean monotony for their inhabitants. Rather, the community is comprised of both attached and semi-attached buildings in multiple stacked configurations. The ground floor of individual units is given over to work space, while the attached upper module provides living quarters and access to roof gardens. Such diverse arrangements are unified by common extensions of the dwellings such as communal gardens and landscaping comprised of drought resistant vegetation. Driven by mechanization, mass production also provides "mass-customization". Yet, sustainable materials temper machine age production.

Der Entwurf von Ecoville basiert auf dem Projekt Portable House des Büros für Mobiles Design und bietet der aufblühenden Kunstszene in Downtown Los Angeles kostengünstige Wohn- und Arbeitsräume. Obwohl Ecoville aus modularen Einheiten besteht, ist diese Standardisierung für die Bewohner nicht gleichbedeutend mit Monotonie. Vielmehr besteht die Gemeinschaft sowohl aus festen wie auch aus halb beweglichen Gebäuden in vielfältigen Kombinationen. Das Erdgeschoss der Häuser wird zum Arbeiten genutzt, während das obere, aufgesetzte Modul als Wohnbereich dient und außerdem Zugang zu den Dachgärten bietet. Diese vielen unterschiedlich aufgebauten Häuser werden optisch durch Gemeinschaftsflächen zusammenfasst, die öffentliche Gärten und Landschaftsgestaltungen mit einer trockenen, widerstandsfähigen Vegetation enthalten. Dank der Technisierung bietet die Massenproduktion heute auch „Massen-Individualisierung" an. Allerdings verbessern widerstandsfähige Materialien die Produkte des Maschinenzeitalters.

swellhouse | venice, ca . usa

D E S I G N : Office of Mobile Design (OMD) / Jennifer Siegal

Through good design, sustainable technology, and environmental materials, the Swellhouse reconstitutes traditional models of prefabricated housing. The components of the house are factory assembled, like a kit of parts, and modules are delivered on site for assembly. The modules are available in a range of configurations to promote the individuality of disparate clientele. Electrical, plumbing, and information technologies are hidden within openings already provided within standardized units. The house's distinct character is derived from its innovative and structurally optimized use of materials. Treated glass panels on the ground floor filter sunlight to provide a cooling effect. Because the glass panels slide, the interior flows into the exterior, uniting the house with its natural landscape. Upstairs, there is a pocket between the outer fiber cement board panels and the inner walls, thus sheltering the interior from the elements while promoting airflow.

Das Swellhouse erneuert dank seines ausgezeichneten Designs, nachhaltiger Technologie und ökologischer Materialien das traditionelle Vorbild des vorgefertigten Hauses. Die Bauteile des Hauses werden in der Fabrik nach dem Baukastenprinzip zusammengesetzt und für die Montage zum Bauplatz geliefert. Um die individuellen Vorstellungen der unterschiedlichen Klientel zu erfüllen, sind die Module in verschiedenen Ausführungen erhältlich. Die Standardbauteile sind mit in Hohlräumen verborgenen Elektro- und Wasseranschlüssen sowie Informationstechnik ausgestattet. Der ausgeprägt eigene Charakter des Hauses beruht auf der innovativen und strukturell optimierten Art und Weise, in der die Materialien eingesetzt werden. Behandelte Glaspaneele im Erdgeschoss filtern das Sonnenlicht und sorgen für Abkühlung. Durch die Glasschiebetüren entsteht ein fließender Übergang vom Innen- zum Außenraum, das Haus vereint sich mit seiner natürlichen Landschaft. Im Obergeschoss befindet sich zwischen den äußeren Betonfaserplatten und den Innenwänden ein Luftloch, so wird der Innenraum vor den Naturgewalten geschützt und gleichzeitig die Luftzirkulation gefördert.

seatrain residence | los angeles, ca . usa

DESIGN: Office of Mobile Design (OMD) / Jennifer Siegal

Constructed from four shipping containers and two grain trailers, the Seatrain Residence's design is literally derived from defunct industrial equipment. The modular components of the house are taken from these utilitarian components, and also echo the project's location in downtown Los Angeles. Not only do the industrial containers reflect the broader industrial landscape of the area, but additional materials like and wooden beams found on the site itself were reused and integrated into the built project. Office of Mobile Design customized these units in collaboration with the needs of the client. The grain trailers were converted into a lap pool and indoor/outdoor koi pond. To designate living and work spaces, specific domestic functions were allocated to each storage unit. Dramatically reconfiguring the original vessels, large glass panels cause natural light to puncture the interior, while also integrating the house within the larger artists' community in which the house is located. The extensive use of recycled materials throughout the house provides both an environmental and affordable alternative to more traditional building methods.

Das Design der Seatrain Residence, die aus vier Schiffscontainern und zwei Getreideanhängern konstruiert wurde, stammt buchstäblich von stillgelegten Industrieanlagen. Die modularen Teile des Gebäudes wurden von diesen Einrichtungen übernommen und reflektieren auch den Standort des Projektes in Downtown Los Angeles. Nicht nur die Industriecontainer spiegeln im weitesten Sinne die Gewerbelandschaft der Gegend wider, sondern auch Materialien wie Wellbleche und Holzbalken, die auf dem Gelände gefunden und nun, in das Projekt integriert, erneut verwendet werden. Das Büro für Mobiles Design stimmte die Wohneinheiten individuell auf die Wünsche und Bedürfnisse der Kunden ab. Die Getreideanhänger wurden zu einem Pool und einem Teich im Innen- und Außenbereich umfunktioniert. Um Wohn- und Arbeitsräume zu definieren, wurden bestimmte häusliche Funktionsbereiche einzelnen Containern zugewiesen. Nach der wirkungsvollen Umgestaltung der Schiffscontainer durchfluten nun große Glasflächen den Innenraum mit natürlichem Licht und gleichzeitig wurde das Gebäude in die größere Künstlergemeinschaft integriert, in der es sich befindet. Durch die ausgiebige Verwendung von recycelten Materialien im ganzen Haus entstand sowohl eine ökologisch durchdachte wie auch finanziell erschwingliche Alternative zu eher traditionellen Baumethoden.

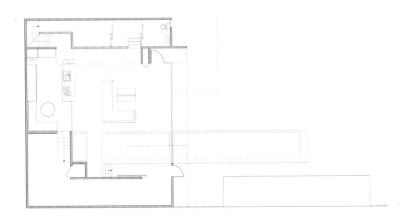

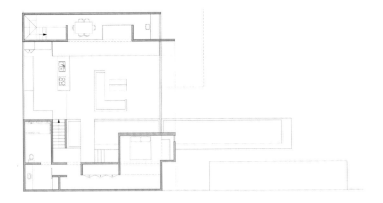

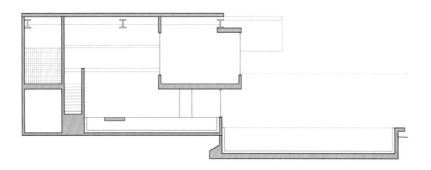

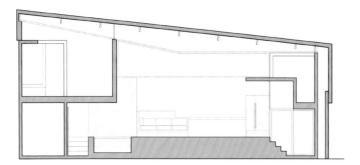

the fish camp | perryville, mo . usa
DESIGN: Rocio Romero

Fish Camp units promote the use of prefabricated structures to return man to nature. In fact, they are specifically designed for recreational use including camping, barbecuing, or simply repose in the wilderness. The concept behind the project is based on a tree house, only one which is portable. Indeed the small structure, with its wooden deck, is ideal for finding relief from city life. But unlike the permanent chalet or cabin, its owners can take their own dwelling to a range of locations. Because the structure can be fashioned above ground, the outdoor experience is no longer hindered by the elements. More permanent than tents typically used for camping, the luxuries of modern life can be brought out-of-doors.

Das Fish Camp wirbt für die Nutzung vorgefertigter Strukturen, um den Menschen wieder einen direkteren Kontakt mit der Natur zu ermöglichen. Tatsächlich wurde das Fish Camp speziell für die Erholung in der Natur entworfen, etwa zum Campen, Grillen oder einfach nur um die Ruhe draußen zu genießen. Das Konzept basiert auf der Idee des Baumhauses, mit dem Unterschied, dass das Fish Camp mobil ist. Die kleine Einheit mit ihrem hölzernen Deck eignet sich in der Tat bestens dazu, Abstand vom Leben in der Stadt zu bekommen. Anders als beim herkömmlichen Ferienhaus oder Chalet können die Besitzer hier ihren Wohnsitz an verschiedene Orte mitnehmen. Da die Konstruktion sich über dem Erdboden befindet, können Umwelteinflüsse das Outdoor-Erlebnis nicht mehr beeinträchtigen. Weil das Fish Camp beständiger ist als das normalerweise beim Camping benutzte Zelt, muss niemand draußen in der Natur auf die Annehmlichkeiten des modernen Lebens verzichten.

house for a sculptor 3 | santa rosa, ca . usa

DESIGN: Sander Architects

For this custom home designed for a sculptor, Sanders Architects took their queue from the artist's work itself. The effect juxtaposes a highly modulated and plastic interior with rough industrial materials cladding the home's exterior. The architect additionally took advantage of the hillside on which the house is located to create a series of unique facades. In addition, the site formulates the house's structure. Displaying a regulated system of structural support, steal framing is left exposed at the rear of the house. Much of the steal frame is also revealed on the interior as a contrast to its otherwise sculptural spaces. Large glazed areas pierce the front façade and provide extensive vistas on the interior. Thanks to extensive windows throughout the home, open and airy spaces provide the ideal atmosphere to exhibit the client's own artwork, thereby displaying the very objects that helped to propel the home's design.

Bei diesem Haus, das für einen Bildhauer wie maßgeschneidert ist, griff das Büro Sander Architects auf eine Arbeit des Künstlers zurück. Dabei wurde auf beeindruckende Weise der modulare und plastische Innenraum des Hauses dem Äußeren gegenübergestellt, das von grob industriell gefertigten Materialien ummantelt wird. Zusätzlich nutzte der Architekt den Vorteil der Hanglage für eine Reihe von einzigartigen Fassaden. Das Gelände definiert auch die Struktur des Gebäudes. Die Trägerstützen weisen ein gleichmäßiges System vor, dessen Stahlrahmenkonstruktion an der Rückseite des Gebäudes sichtbar bleibt. Große Teile dieser Konstruktion sind auch im Inneren zu erkennen, wo sie einen Kontrast zu den anderen plastischen Räumen bilden. Riesige verglaste Flächen durchbohren die vordere Fassade und bieten weiträumige Einblicke ins Innere. Dank der großflächigen Fenster im ganzen Haus sorgen offene und luftig wirkende Räume für das perfekte Ambiente, um die Kunstwerke des Bauherren auszustellen. Darunter sind auch diejenigen Objekte, auf die das Design des Gebäudes zurückgeht.

haus sunoko | memmingen . germany

DESIGN: SoHo Architektur und Stadtplanung

The unusual property size of 230 meters long and only 10 meters wide and a very lean cost-calculation were the decisive factors in the form for the "house on stilts" in the southern German city of Memmingen. The unspoiled landscape with a few farms, fields, and allotments for small gardens make extremely large window openings possible in the façade of the two-story building. These gorgeous panoramas were also a consideration when designing the floor plan. The living room and bedrooms are found on the two front faces of the house which is clad in Plexiglas-corrugated panels. The open kitchen, bathroom, guest room, and bath are concentric in the house, whereas a spacious dining area with a view of the landscape is found to east. A large, open space combines the upper and the lower floors. The floor, exterior walls, and ceiling elements are completely ready-made in modular style of construction and point by point set on girders with 40 centimeters distance to the ground; construction was therefore able to be completed in a single day. Since there was no basement, it was replaced by a small shed outside. The changing light conditions alter the appearance of the outer skin by various nuances and make the contrast between modern architecture and rural idyll even more interesting.

Die außergewöhnliche Grundstücksfläche von 230 Meter Länge auf nur 10 Meter Breite und ein knapp bemessenes Budget waren entscheidende Formgeber für das „Haus auf Stelzen" im süddeutschen Memmingen. Die unverbaute Landschaft mit vereinzelten Bauernhöfen, Feldern und Schrebergärten ermöglicht extrem große Fensteröffnungen in der Fassade des zweistöckigen Gebäudes. Auch der Grundriss reagiert auf diese traumhaften Aussichten. An den beiden Stirnseiten des mit Plexiglas-Wellplatten verkleideten Hauses befinden sich Wohn- und Schlafräume. Mittig angeordnet sind die offene Küche, WC, Gästezimmer und Bad, während nach Osten hin ein großzügiger Essplatz freie Sicht in die Natur bietet. Ein Luftraum verbindet das obere mit dem unteren Stockwerk. Fußboden-, Außenwand- und Deckenelemente sind komplett in Holzrahmen-Bauweise vorgefertigt und vor Ort punktweise auf Stahlträgern mit 40 Zentimeter Abstand zum Boden gelagert, wodurch der Bau innerhalb eines einzigen Tages aufgestellt werden konnte. Der fehlende Keller wird durch einen kleinen Schuppen ersetzt. Wechselnde Lichtverhältnisse verändern das Erscheinungsbild der Außenhaut durch unterschiedliche Farbnuancen und erzeugen eine zusätzliche Spannung zwischen moderner Architektur und ländlicher Idylle.

atelier in a mountain, chanayu room | yamagata . japan

DESIGN: Toshihiko Suzuki

Toshihiko Suzuki has carefully redefined traditional Japanese architecture with the help of modern technology and thus given it a kind of face lift. For the Chanayu room, the designer once again dedicates himself to the subject of the preparation of tea and refers to ancient traditions and customs. The 2 x 2 meter cube is raised 30 centimeters off the ground and offers room for an integrated fire place. The sources of light, which bathe the room in a gentle light, are set into the honeycomb-shaped wall panels made of aluminum and which create delicate patterns that seem to move slightly on the walls. The canopy, an aluminum construction made of precisely cut semi-circles, which can be constructed and carried by two people, covers the streamlined trailer and the Chanayu room. The architect and designer had to be sure that the atelier in the mountains, as this design is called, can be completely disassembled due to the predetermined building requirements. After it has been disassembled, there should be no indications of its previous existence on the site.

Die traditionelle japanische Architektur wird von Toshihiko Suzuki mit Hilfe moderner Technologie behutsam neu definiert und bekommt so eine Art Facelifting. Erneut widmet sich der Designer beim Chanayu Room dem Thema der Teezubereitung und bezieht sich hierbei auf althergebrachte Traditionen und Bräuche. Der 2 auf 2 Meter große Kubus erhebt sich 30 Zentimeter über dem Boden und bietet so Platz für einen integrierten Feuerplatz. In die wabenförmigen Wandpaneele aus Aluminium sind Lichtquellen eingesetzt, die den Innenraum in ein sanftes Licht tauchen und ein zartes Muster an den Wänden erzeugen, das sich kontinuierlich leicht zu bewegen scheint. Das Schutzdach, eine Aluminiumkonstruktion aus präzise geschnittenen Halbbögen, die von zwei Personen allein zusammengebaut und auch getragen werden kann, überspannt den stromlinienförmigen Wohnanhänger und den Chanayu Room. Aufgrund der vorgegebenen Baubedingungen musste der Architekt und Designer sicherstellen, dass das „Atelier in den Bergen", wie dieser Entwurf auch genannt wird, komplett deinstallierbar ist. Nach dem Abbau weist nichts mehr auf seine ehemalige Existenz am Standort hin.

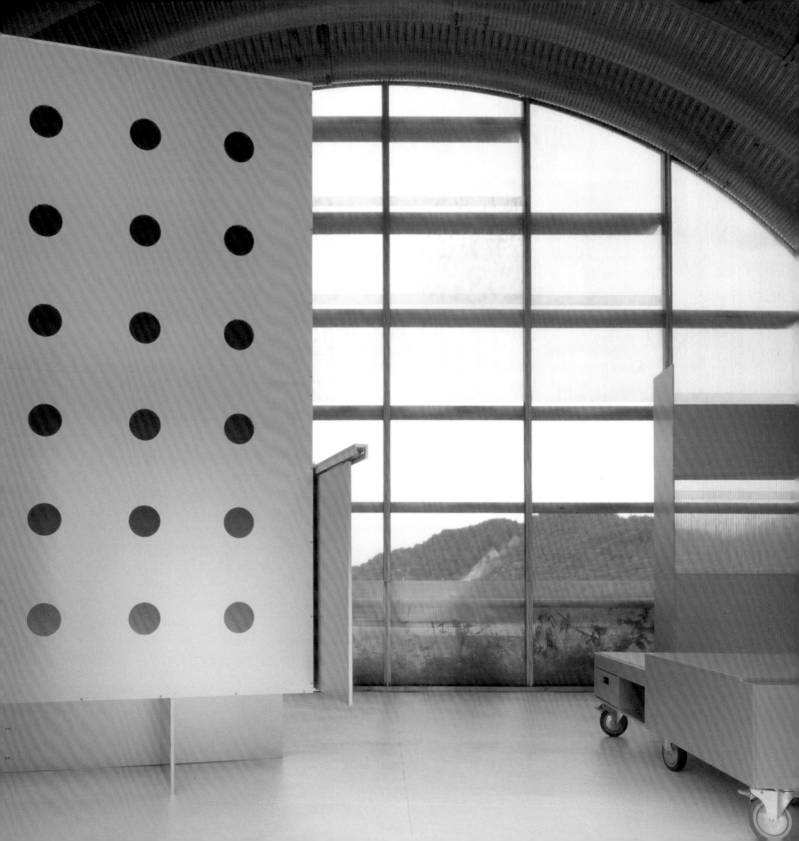

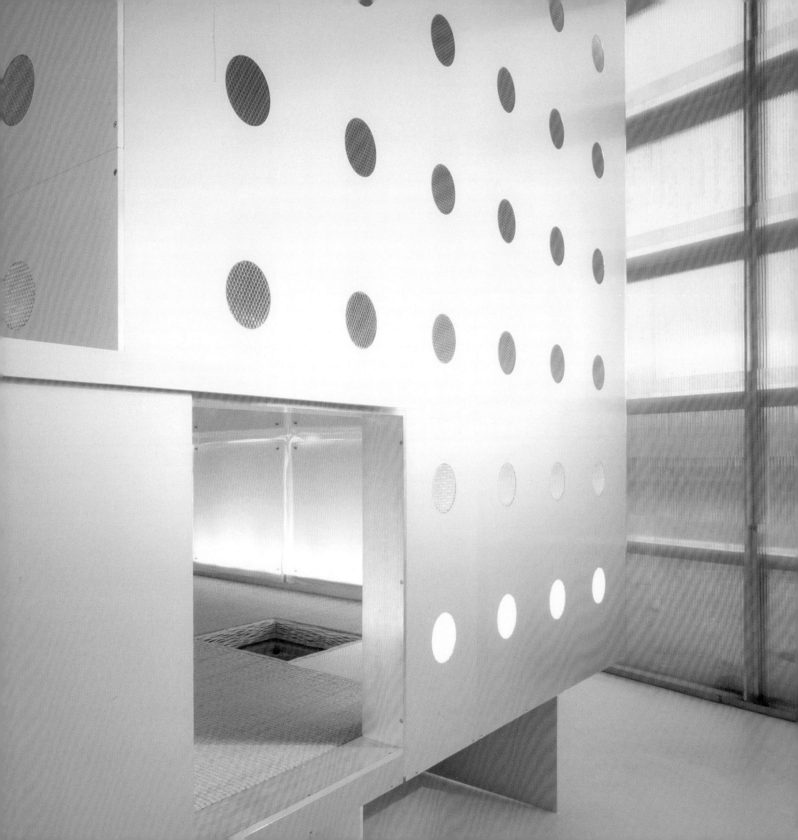

mobile ichijyo | variable
DESIGN: Toshihiko Suzuki

The art of tea preparation is a time honored tradition in Japanese culture. The mobile ichijyo is dedicated to this procedure. One can dedicate oneself to this meditative procedure in a very small space, to be more precise, in a single transportable room. Toshihiko Suzuki's design strongly reminds one of a simple paper lantern. A flat aluminum box is pulled apart much like an accordion and constitutes the setting for the frame, which become floor and ceiling areas for the light mobile ichijyo. In between there is a curtain made of white mosquito netting which separates the interior from the outside world. The floor of the mobile ichijyo is covered with a tatami mat, which offers just enough space to sleep upon. Another slightly altered form of this design is a creation of what is seemingly arbitrarily arranged cables, pipes, and material which form a similar intimate, secluded interior.

Die Kunst der Teezubereitung ist eine jahrhundertelang gepflegte Tradition in der japanischen Kultur. Genau diesem Prozedere ist das mobile ichijyo gewidmet. Auf kleinstem Raum, genauer gesagt in einem einzigen transportablen Raum, kann man sich diesem meditativen Vorgang widmen. Der Entwurf des Designers Toshihiko Suzuki ist stark an die Optik einer einfachen Papierlaterne oder eines Lampions angelehnt. Ein flacher Aluminiumkasten wird einer Ziehharmonika gleich auseinander gezogen und bildet den Rahmen für das Gestell, wird Boden- und Deckenfläche für das leichte mobile. Dazwischen entfaltet sich ein Vorhang aus weißem Moskitonetz, der den Innenraum von der Außenwelt trennt. Der Boden des mobile ichijyo ist mit einer Tatami-Matte bedeckt, deren Größe gerade ausreichend Fläche zum Schlafen bietet. Eine weitere abgewandelte Form dieses ersten Entwurfs ist ein Gebilde aus willkürlich angeordnet scheinenden Kabeln, Röhren und Stoff, die einen ähnlich intimen, zurückgezogenen Innenraum formen.

heidis | kiens . italy
DESIGN: Matteo Thun

One might think that the architect, Matteo Thun, from Milan is joking with the name of his pre-fabricated house. One immediately thinks of the typical clichés associated with this name: the Alps, barns, farms, and pristine countryside. It is true that Heidis are not high-tech houses, but are completely built of wood, if one overlooks stonewalled segments. Nevertheless, they still cannot be considered a wooden cabin in the Alps. The appearance of the "zero energy house" is optimally integrated into the landscape and nature with its curved rooftops, the windowless north side and a glass façade on the south side. The architect himself also speaks of a type of "light shutter", which opens the house to the sun and thus to its warmth. The effective energy-storing characteristics of the wood enable an efficient energy supply, because wood not only projects warmth optically. The interior is divided by a massive wooden stand construction made of spruce, in which each everyday function receives its own fixed place. Heidis are available in 6 different sizes. The cross-section of the curved arc always remains the same, only the length varies according to the desired size of the house.

Fast könnte man meinen, dass der Mailänder Architekt Matteo Thun mit dem Namen seines Fertighauses provozieren möchte. Sofort denkt man an die typischen Klischees, die mit diesem Namen verbunden sind: Alpen, Stadel, Höfe und unberührte Landschaften. In der Tat ist Heidis kein Hightech-Haus, sondern konsequent in Holz gebaut, wenn man von den gemauerten Wangen absieht. Dennoch kann von einer Holzhütte in den Alpen keine Rede sein. Das Erscheinungsbild des Passivhauses integriert sich durch seinen geschwungenen Dachrücken, die fensterlose Nordseite und eine Glasfassade auf der Südseite optimal in Landschaft und Natur. Der Architekt selbst spricht auch von einer „Lichtklappe", die den Haushügel zur Sonne und damit zur Wärme hin öffnet. Die guten speicherwirksamen Eigenschaften des Werkstoffs Holz ermöglichen eine effiziente Energieversorgung, denn Holz strahlt nicht nur optisch Wärme aus. Der Innenraum ist unveränderbar durch eine massive Holzständerkonstruktion aus Fichte gegliedert, wobei jede Alltagsfunktion einen festen Platz erhält. Heidis ist in 6 verschiedenen Baugrößen erhältlich. Der Querschnitt des geschwungenen Lichtbogens bleibt dabei immer gleich, lediglich die Länge variiert je nach gewünschter Größe des Hauses.

o sole mio | griffen . austria
DESIGN: Matteo Thun

The sun with its warmth and light is object of desire for every house, says Matteo Thun, the architect of this modular house system. With its transparent glass façade, O' sole mio uses the energy of the sun and is not dependent on solar collectors and heat pumps thanks to the orientation to the sun. The cross-section of the awning house—formative for the entire appearance—reminds one of the mountain cabins of the Alpine Association around 1900. The complex building system is solid and designed with high standards of aesthetics and functional durability. The type cross-section of O' sole mio offers numerous combination possibilities and allows the freedom to build a unique house, according to one's own individual creativity. The house has rather simple, straight lines and is impressive with its clear appearance made of larch wood and glass. The materials communicate lightness and transparency; in combination the latest integrated technology and design, it offers the greatest quality of living. The company, Griffner Fertighaus AG, produces and distributes the serial prefabrication of O' sole mio.

Die Sonne mit ihrer Wärme und ihrem Licht ist für jedes Haus das Objekt der Begierde, meint Matteo Thun, der Architekt dieses Fertighaussystems. Mit seiner transparenten Glasfassade nutzt O' sole mio die Energie der Sonne und kommt dank der „sonnengeeichten" Ausrichtung des Gebäudes ohne Kollektoren und Wärmepumpen aus. Der Querschnitt des Sonnensegelhauses – prägend für das Gesamterscheinungsbild – lehnt sich stark an die Bergsteigerhütten des Alpenvereins um 1900 an. Das vielschichtige Bausystem ist solide und mit dem Anspruch an ästhetische und funktionale Dauerhaftigkeit konzipiert. Nach dem „Salamiprinzip" bietet der Typenquerschnitt von O' sole mio unzählige Kombinationsmöglichkeiten und gestattet so die Freiheit, je nach individueller Kreativität ein einmaliges Haus zu bauen. Dabei präsentiert sich das Gebäude schnörkellos, geradlinig und beeindruckt durch sein klares Bild aus Lärchenholz und Glas. Die Materialien vermitteln Leichtigkeit und Transparenz; in Kombination mit integrierter neuester Technologie und Design bieten sie höchste Wohnqualität. Die Griffner-Fertighaus AG produziert und vertreibt die serielle Voranfertigung von O' sole mio.

index & photo credits

cover photo: Steffen Jänicke
backcover photo: Sharon Risedorph

introduction: Olafur Mathiesen 4 l, 6 r
Myrzik + Jarisch Fotografen 4 r
Alejandro Dumay 5 l
Steffen Jänicke 5 r
Gaston Wicky 6 l
www.digiflash.at 7 l
Nacasa & Partners 7 r

imprint

Bibliographic Information published by Die Deutsche Bibliothek
Die Deutsche Bibliothek lists this publication in the Deutsche
Nationalbibliografie; detailed bibliographic data are available in the
internet at http://dnb.ddb.de

ISBN-10: 3-89986-055-1
ISBN-13: 978-3-89986-055-9

1st edition

Printed in Austria

Editors | Martin Nicholas Kunz, Michelle Galindo
Texts (page) | Katharina Feuer (14, 24, 30, 36, 40, 46, 50, 64, 76, 78, 82, 84, 88,
92, 96, 100, 106, 116, 122, 118, 150, 154, 160, 162, 164), Sean Weiss (8, 20, 56,
60, 66, 70, 74, 112, 126, 130, 132, 134, 142, 144)
Translations | Ade Team
Layout | Michelle Galindo
Digital Imaging | Jeremy Ellington
Printing | Vorarlberger Verlagsanstalt AG, Dornbirn, Austria

Martin Nicholas Kunz

1957 born in Hollywood.
Founder of fusion publishing
creating content for architecture, design, travel and
lifestyle publications.

Michelle Galindo

1982 born in Los Angeles.
Studies of architecture at
Woodbury University, Los
Angeles and editor of several
architecture guide books.

other books:

best designed hotels:
asia pacific
americas
europe I (urban)
europe II (countryside)

best designed
swiss hotels
hotel pools
outdoor living

best designed wellness hotels:
asia pacific
americas
europe
africa & middle East

All books are released in
German and English

avedition GmbH
Königsallee 57 | 71638 Ludwigsburg | Germany
p +49-7141-1477391 | f +49-7141-1477399
www.avedition.com | kontakt@avedition.com